Strike Sparks

Strike Sparks

Selected Poems 1980–2002

Sharon Olds

NEW YORK   ALFRED A. KNOPF   2013

THIS IS A BORZOI BOOK
PUBLISHED BY ALFRED A. KNOPF

Copyright © 2004 by Sharon Olds

www.aaknopf.com

Knopf, Borzoi Books, and the colophon are registered trademarks
of Random House, Inc.

Grateful acknowledgment is made to the University of Pittsburgh
Press for permission to reprint "Indictment of Senior Officials,"
"The Sisters of Sexual Treasure," "Station," "Monarchs," "Infinite
Bliss," "The Language of the Brag," "The Talk," and "I Could Not
Tell" from *Satan Says* by Sharon Olds. Copyright © 1980 by Sharon
Olds. Reprinted by permission of the University of Pittsburgh Press.

All other poems in this collection have been previously published in
the following Alfred A. Knopf works: *The Dead and the Living* (1984);
The Gold Cell (1987); *The Father* (1992); *The Wellspring* (1996);
Blood, Tin, Straw (1999); *The Unswept Room* (2002)

Library of Congress Cataloging-in-Publication Data
Olds, Sharon.
    Strike sparks : selected poems, 1980–2002 / Sharon Olds.—1st ed.
    p. cm.
    ISBN 1-4000-4278-X.—ISBN 0-375-71076-0 (pbk.)
    I. Title.

PS3565.L34A6 2004
811'.5—dc2   2004044150

Manufactured in the United States of America
Published October 4, 2004
Reprinted Five Times
Seventh Paperback Printing, April 2013

For Phil and Franny

I
take them up like the male and female
paper dolls and bang them together
at the hip, like chips of flint, as if to
strike sparks from them, I say
Do what you are going to do, and I will tell about it.

Contents

from *The Gold Cell*   *(1987)*

from *The Father*   *(1992)*

from *The Wellspring*   *(1996)*

from *The Unswept Room*   *(2002)*

from *Satan Says*

Indictment of Senior Officers

In the hallway above the pit of the stairwell
my sister and I would meet, at night,
eyes and hair dark, bodies
like twins in the dark. We did not talk of
the two who had brought us there, like generals,
for their own reasons. We sat, buddies in cold
war, her living body the proof of
my living body, our backs to the mild
shell hole of the stairs, down which
we would have to go, knowing nothing
but what we had learned there,

                    so that now
when I think of my sister, the holes of the needles
in her hips and in the creases of her elbows,
and the marks from the doctor husband's beatings,
and the scars of the operations, I feel the
rage of a soldier standing over the body of
someone sent to the front lines
without training
or a weapon.

The Sisters of Sexual Treasure

As soon as my sister and I got out of our
mother's house, all we wanted to
do was fuck, obliterate
her tiny sparrow body and narrow
grasshopper legs. The men's bodies
were like our father's body! The massive
hocks, flanks, thighs, male
structure of the hips, knees, calves—
we could have him there, the steep forbidden
buttocks, backs of the knees, the cock
in our mouth, ah the cock in our mouth.
                    Like explorers who
discover a lost city, we went
nuts with joy, undressed the men
slowly and carefully, as if
uncovering buried artifacts that
proved our theory of the lost culture:
that if Mother said it wasn't there,
it was there.

Station

Coming in off the dock after writing,
I approached the house,
and saw your fine grandee face
lit by a lamp with a parchment shade
the color of flame.

An elegant hand on your beard. Your tapered
eyes found me on the lawn. You looked
as the lord looks down from a narrow window
and you are descended from lords. Calmly, with no
hint of shyness, you examined me,
the wife who runs out on the dock to write
as soon as one of the children is in bed,
leaving the other to you.

               Your thin
mouth, flexible as an archer's bow,
did not curve. We spent a long moment
in the truth of our situation, the poems
heavy as poached game hanging from my hands.

Monarchs

(for P. W.)

All morning, as I sit, thinking of you,
the Monarchs are passing. Seven stories up,
to the left of the river, they are making their way
south, their wings the dry red of
your hands like butchers' hands, the raised
veins of their wings like your scars.
I could scarcely feel your massive rough
palms on me, your touch was so light,
the chapped scrape of an insect's leg
across my breast. No one had ever
touched me before. I didn't know enough to
open my legs, but felt your thighs,
feathered with red, gold hairs,
    opening
between my legs
like a pair of wings.
The hinged print of my blood on your thighs—
a winged creature, pinned there—
and then you left, as you were to leave
over and over, the butterflies moving
in masses past my window, floating
south to their transformation, crossing over
borders in the night, the diffuse blood-red
cloud of them, my body under yours,
the beauty and silence of the great migrations.

Infinite Bliss

When I first saw snow cover the air
with its delicate hoofprints, I said I would never
live where it did not snow, and when
the first man tore his way into me,
and tore up the passageway,
and came to the small room, and pulled the
curtain aside that I might enter, I knew I could
never live apart from them
again, the strange race with their massive
bloodied hooves. Today we lay in our
small bedroom, dark gold with
reflected snow, and while the flakes climbed
delicately down the sky, you
came into me, pressing aside
the curtain, revealing the small room,
dark gold with reflected snow,
where we lay, and where you entered me and
pressed the curtain aside, revealing
the small room, dark gold with
reflected snow, where we lay.

The Language of the Brag

I have wanted excellence in the knife-throw,
I have wanted to use my exceptionally strong and accurate arms
and my straight posture and quick electric muscles
to achieve something at the center of a crowd,
the blade piercing the bark deep,
the haft slowly and heavily vibrating like the cock.

I have wanted some epic use for my excellent body,
some heroism, some American achievement
beyond the ordinary for my extraordinary self,
magnetic and tensile, I have stood by the sandlot
and watched the boys play.

I have wanted courage, I have thought about fire
and the crossing of waterfalls, I have dragged around

my belly big with cowardice and safety,
stool charcoal from the iron pills,
huge breasts leaking colostrum,
legs swelling, hands swelling,
face swelling and reddening, hair
falling out, inner sex
stabbed again and again with pain like a knife.
I have lain down.

I have lain down and sweated and shaken
and passed blood and shit and water and
slowly alone in the center of a circle I have
passed the new person out
and they have lifted the new person free of the act
and wiped the new person free of that
language of blood like praise all over the body.

I have done what you wanted to do, Walt Whitman,
Allen Ginsberg, I have done this thing,
I and the other women this exceptional
act with the exceptional heroic body,
this giving birth, this glistening verb,
and I am putting my proud American boast
right here with the others.

The Talk

In the sunless wooden room at noon
the mother had a talk with her daughter.
The rudeness could not go on, the meanness
to her little brother, the selfishness.
The eight-year-old sat on the bed
in the corner of the room, her irises distilled as
the last drops of something, her firm
face melting, reddening,
silver flashes in her eyes like distant
bodies of water glimpsed through woods.
She took it and took it and broke, crying out
I hate being a person! diving
into the mother
as if
into
a deep pond—and she cannot swim,
the child cannot swim.

I Could Not Tell

I could not tell I had jumped off that bus,
that bus in motion, with my child in my arms,
because I did not know it. I believed my own story:
I had fallen, or the bus had started up
when I had one foot in the air.

I would not remember the tightening of my jaw,
the irk that I'd missed my stop, the step out
into the air, the clear child
gazing about her in the air as I plunged
to one knee on the street, scraped it, twisted it,
the bus skidding to a stop, the driver
jumping out, my daughter laughing
Do it again.

        I have never done it
again. I have been very careful.
I have kept an eye on that nice young mother
who lightly leapt
off the moving vehicle
onto the stopped street, her life
in her hands, her life's life in her hands.

from *The Dead and the Living*

Ideographs

(a photograph of China, 1905)

The handmade scaffolds, boards in the form of
ideographs the size of a person
lean against a steep wall
of dressed stone. One is the simple
shape of a man. The man on it
is asleep, his arms nailed to the wood.
No timber is wasted; his fingertips
curl in at the very end of the plank
as a child's hand opens in sleep.
The other man is awake—he looks
directly at us. He is fixed to a more
complex scaffold, a diagonal crosspiece
pointing one arm up, one down,
and his legs are bent, the spikes through his ankles
holding them up, off the ground,
his knees cocked, the folds of his robe flowing
sideways as if he were suspended in the air
in flight, his naked legs bared.
They await execution, tilted to the wall
as you'd prop up a tool until you needed it.
They'll be shouldered up over the crowd and
carried through the screaming. The sleeper will wake.
The twisted one will fly above the faces, his
garment rippling.
Here there is still the backstage quiet,
the shadow at the bottom of the wall, the props
leaning in the grainy half-dusk.
He looks at us in the silence. He says
Save me, there is still time.

Photograph of the Girl

The girl sits on the hard ground,
the dry pan of Russia, in the drought
of 1921, stunned,
eyes closed, mouth open,
raw, hot wind blowing
sand in her face. Hunger and puberty
are taking her together. She leans on a sack,
layers of clothes fluttering in the heat,
the new radius of her arm curved.
She cannot be not beautiful, but she is
starving. Each day she grows thinner, and her bones
grow longer, porous. The caption says
she is going to starve to death that winter
with millions of others. Deep in her body
the ovaries let out her first eggs,
golden as drops of grain.

Race Riot, Tulsa, 1921

The blazing white shirts of the white men
are blanks on the page, looking at them is like
looking at the sun, you could go blind.
Under the snouts of the machine guns,
the dark glowing skin of the women and
men going to jail. You can look at the
gleaming horse chestnuts of their faces the whole day.
All but one descend from the wood
back of the flatbed truck. He lies,
shoes pointed North and South,
knuckles curled under on the splintered slats,
head thrown back as if he is in
a field, his face tilted up
toward the sky, to get the sun on it, to
darken it more and more toward the color of the human.

Of All the Dead That Have Come
to Me, This Once

I have never written against the dead. I feel as
if I would open my shirt to them, the
cones still making sugary milk, but when

Grandfather's 14-carat pocketwatch
came in by air over the Rockies,
over the shorn yellow of the fields
and the winter rivers, with Grandmother's blank
face pressed against his name in the back,

I thought of how he put the empty
plate in front of my sister, turned out
the lights after supper, sat in the ashen
room with the fire, the light of the flames
flashing, in his glass eye, in that
cabin where he taught my father his notion
of what a man's life was, and I said

No. I said, Let this one be dead.
Let the fall he made through the glass roof,
splintering, turning, the companion shanks and
slices of glass in the air, be his last
appearance here.

Miscarriage

When I was a month pregnant, the great
clots of blood appeared in the pale
green swaying water of the toilet,
brick red like black in the salty
translucent brine, like forms of life
appearing, jellyfish with the clear-cut
shapes of fungi.

That was the only appearance made
by that child, the rough, scalloped shapes
falling slowly. A month later
our son was conceived, and I never went back
to mourn the one who came as far as the
sill with its information: that we could
botch something, you and I. All wrapped in
purple it floated away, like a messenger
put to death for bearing bad news.

My Father Snoring

Deep in the night, I would hear it through the wall—
my father snoring, the dense, tuneless
clotted mucus rising in his nose and
falling, like coils of seaweed a wave
brings in and takes back. The clogged roar
filled the house. Even down in the kitchen,
in the drawers, the knives and forks hummed
with that distant throbbing. But in my room,
next to theirs, it was so loud
I could feel myself inside his body,
lifted on the knotted rope of his life
and lowered again, into the narrow
ragged well, its amber walls
slick around my torso, the smell of bourbon
pungent as sputum. He lay like a felled
beast all night and sounded his thick
buried stoppered call, like a cry for
help. And no one ever came:
there were none of his kind around there anywhere.

The Moment

When I saw the red Egyptian stain,
I went down into the house to find you, Mom—
past the grandfather clock, with its huge
ochre moon, past the burnt
sienna woodwork, rubbed and glazed.
I went lower and lower down into the
body of the house, down below
the level of the earth,
I found you there
where I had never found you, by the old sink,
your hands to the elbow in soapy water,
and above your head, the blazing windows
at the surface of the ground.
You looked up from the zinc tub,
a short haggard pretty woman
of forty, one week divorced.
"I've got my period, Mom," I said,
and saw your face abruptly break open and
glow with joy. "Baby," you said,
coming toward me, hands out and
covered with tiny delicate bubbles like seeds.

The Connoisseuse of Slugs

When I was a connoisseuse of slugs
I would part the ivy leaves, and look for the
naked jelly of those greenish creatures,
translucent strangers glistening along
the stones, slowly, their gelatinous bodies
at my mercy. Made mostly of water, they would shrivel
to nothing if they were sprinkled with salt,
but I was not interested in that. What I liked
was to draw aside the ivy, breathe
the odor of the wall, and stand there in silence
until the slug forgot I was there
and sent its antennae up out of its
head, the glimmering umber horns
rising like telescopes, until finally the
sensitive knobs would pop out the ends,
unerring and intimate. Years later,
when I first saw a naked man,
I gasped with pleasure to see that quiet
mystery reenacted, the slow
elegant being coming out of hiding and
gleaming in the powdery air, eager and so
trusting you could weep.

New Mother

A week after our child was born,
you cornered me in the spare room
and we sank down on the bed.
You kissed me and kissed me, my milk undid its
burning slipknot through my nipples,
soaking my shirt. All week I had smelled of milk,
fresh milk, sour. I began to throb:
my sex had been torn easily as cloth by the
crown of her head, I'd been cut with a knife and
sewn, the stitches pulling at my skin—and the
first time you're broken, you don't know
you'll be healed again, better than before.
I lay in fear and blood and milk
while you kissed and kissed me, your lips hot and swollen
as a teenage boy's, your sex dry and big,
all of you so tender, you hung over me,
over the nest of the stitches, over the
splitting and tearing, with the patience of someone who
finds a wounded animal in the woods
and stays with it, not leaving its side
until it is whole, until it can run again.

Sex Without Love

How do they do it, the ones who make love
without love? Formal as dancers,
gliding over each other like ice-skaters
over the ice, fingers hooked
inside each other's bodies, faces
red as steak, wine, wet as the
children at birth whose mothers are going to
give them away. How do they come to the
come to the   come to the   God   come to the
still waters, and not love
the one who came there with them, heat
rising slowly as steam off their joined
skin? I guess they are the true religious,
the purists, the pros, the ones who will not
accept a false Messiah, love the
priest instead of the God. They do not
mistake the partner for their own pleasure,
they are like great runners: they know they are alone
with the road surface, the cold, the wind,
the fit of their shoes, their overall cardio-
vascular health—just factors, like the other
in the bed, and not their truth, which is
the single body alone in the universe
against its own best time.

Ecstasy

As we made love for the third day,
cloudy and dark, as we did not stop but went
into it, and into it, and
did not hesitate and did not hold back we
rose through the air, until we were up above
timber line. The lake lay,
icy and silver, the surface shirred,
reflecting nothing. The black rocks
lifted around it, into the grainy
sepia air, the patches of snow
brilliant white, and even though we
did not know where we were, we could not
speak the language, we could hardly see, we
did not stop, rising with the black
rocks to the black hills, the black
mountains rising from the hills. Resting
on the crest of the mountains, one huge
cloud with scalloped edges of blazing
evening light, we did not turn back,
we stayed with it, even though we were
far beyond what we knew, we rose
into the grain of the cloud, even though we were
frightened, the air hollow, even though
nothing grew there, even though it is a
place from which no one has ever come back.

Exclusive

(for my daughter)

I lie on the beach, watching you
as you lie on the beach, memorizing you
against the time when you will not be with me:
your empurpled lips, swollen in the sun
and smooth as the inner lips of a shell;
your biscuit-gold skin, glazed and
faintly pitted, like the surface of a biscuit;
the serious knotted twine of your hair.
I have loved you instead of anyone else,
loved you as a way of loving no one else,
every separate grain of your body
building the god, as you were built within me,
a sealed world. What if from your lips
I had learned the love of other lips,
from your starred, gummed lashes the love of
other lashes, from your shut, quivering
eyes the love of other eyes,
from your body the bodies,
from your life the lives?
Today I see it is there to be learned from you:
to love what I do not own.

Rite of Passage

As the guests arrive at our son's party
they gather in the living room—
short men, men in first grade
with smooth jaws and chins.
Hands in pockets, they stand around
jostling, jockeying for place, small fights
breaking out and calming. One says to another
How old are you? —Six. —I'm seven. —So?
They eye each other, seeing themselves
tiny in the other's pupils. They clear their
throats a lot, a room of small bankers,
they fold their arms and frown. *I could beat you
up*, a seven says to a six,
the midnight cake, round and heavy as a
turret, behind them on the table. My son,
freckles like specks of nutmeg on his cheeks,
chest narrow as the balsa keel of a
model boat, long hands
cool and thin as the day they guided him
out of me, speaks up as a host
for the sake of the group.
We could easily kill a two-year-old,
he says in his clear voice. The other
men agree, they clear their throats
like Generals, they relax and get down to
playing war, celebrating my son's life.

Brushing out our daughter's brown
silken hair before the mirror
I see the grey gleaming on my head,
the silver-haired servant behind her. Why is it
just as we begin to go
they begin to arrive, the fold in my neck
clarifying as the fine bones of her
hips sharpen? As my skin shows
its dry pitting, she opens like a moist
precise flower on the tip of a cactus;
as my last chances to bear a child
are falling through my body, the duds among them,
her full purse of eggs, round and
firm as hard-boiled yolks, is about
to snap its clasp. I brush her tangled
fragrant hair at bedtime. It's an old
story—the oldest we have on our planet—
the story of replacement.

The Missing Boy

(for Etan Patz)

Every time we take the bus
my son sees the picture of the missing boy.
He looks at it like a mirror—the dark
straw hair, the pale skin,
the blue eyes, the electric-blue sneakers with
slashes of jagged gold. But of course that
kid is little, only six and a half,
an age when things can happen to you,
when you're not really safe, and our son is seven,
practically fully grown—why, he would
tower over that kid if they could
find him and bring him right here on this bus and
stand them together. He holds to the pole,
wishing for that, the tape on the poster
gleaming over his head, beginning to
melt at the center and curl at the edges as it
ages. At night, when I put him to bed,
my son holds my hand tight
and says he's sure that kid's all right,
nothing to worry about, he just
hopes he's getting the food he likes,
not just any old food, but the food
he likes the most, the food he is used to.

Bestiary

Nostrils flared, ears pricked,
our son asks me if people can mate with
animals. I say it hardly
ever happens. He frowns, fur and
skin and hooves and teeth and tails
whirling in his brain. You *could* do it,
he says, and we talk about elephants
and parakeets, until we are rolling on the
floor, laughing like hyenas. Too late,
I remember love—I backtrack
and try to slip it in, but that is
not what he means. Seven years old,
he is into hydraulics, pulleys, doors
which fly open in the side of the body,
entrances, exits. Flushed, panting,
hot for physics, he thinks about lynxes,
eagles, pythons, mosquitoes, girls,
casting a glittering eye of use
over creation, wanting to know
exactly how the world was made to receive him.

The One Girl at the Boys' Party

When I take our girl to the swimming party
I set her down among the boys. They tower
and bristle, she stands there smooth and sleek,
her math scores unfolding in the air around her.
They will strip to their suits, her body hard and
indivisible as a prime number,
they'll plunge in the deep end, she'll subtract
her height from ten feet, divide it into
hundreds of gallons of water, the numbers
bouncing in her mind like molecules of chlorine
in the bright-blue pool. When they climb out,
her ponytail will hang its pencil lead
down her back, her narrow silk suit
with hamburgers and french fries printed on it
will glisten in the brilliant air, and they will
see her sweet face, solemn and
sealed, a factor of one, and she will
see their eyes, two each,
their legs, two each, and the curves of their sexes,
one each, and in her head she'll be doing her
wild multiplying, as the drops
sparkle and fall to the power of a thousand from her body.

from *The Gold Cell*

Summer Solstice, New York City

By the end of the longest day of the year he could not stand it,
he went up the iron stairs through the roof of the building
and over the soft, tarry surface
to the edge, put one leg over the complex green tin cornice
and said if they came a step closer that was it.
Then the huge machinery of the earth began to work for his life,
the cops came in their suits blue-grey as the sky on a cloudy evening,
and one put on a bulletproof vest, a
dense shell around his own life,
life of his children's father, in case
the man was armed, and one, slung with a
rope like the sign of his bounden duty,
came up out of a hole in the top of the neighboring building
like the hole they say is in the top of the head,
and began to lurk toward the man who wanted to die.
The tallest cop approached him directly,
softly, slowly, talking to him, talking, talking,
while the man's leg hung over the lip of the next world
and the crowd gathered in the street, silent, and the
hairy net with its implacable grid was
unfolded, near the curb, and spread out, and
stretched as the sheet is prepared to receive at a birth.
Then they all came a little closer
where he squatted next to his death, his shirt
glowing its milky glow like something
growing in a dish at night in the dark in a lab and then
everything stopped
as his body jerked and he
stepped down from the parapet and went toward them
and they closed on him, I thought they were going to
beat him up, as a mother whose child has been
lost might scream at the child when it's found, they

took him by the arms and held him up and
leaned him against the wall of the chimney and the
tall cop lit a cigarette
in his own mouth, and gave it to him, and
then they all lit cigarettes, and the
red, glowing ends burned like the
tiny campfires we lit at night
back at the beginning of the world.

On the Subway

The young man and I face each other.
His feet are huge, in black sneakers
laced with white in a complex pattern like a
set of intentional scars. We are stuck on
opposite sides of the car, a couple of
molecules stuck in a rod of energy
rapidly moving through darkness. He has
or my white eye imagines he has
the casual cold look of a mugger,
alert under lowered eyelids. He is wearing
red, like the inside of the body
exposed. I am wearing old fur, the
whole skin of an animal taken
and used. I look at his unknown face,
he looks at my grandmother's coat, and I don't
know if I am in his power—
he could take my coat so easily, my
briefcase, my life—
or if he is in my power, the way I am
living off his life, eating the steak
he may not be eating, as if I am taking
the food from his mouth. And he is black
and I am white, and without meaning or
trying to I must profit from our history,
the way he absorbs the murderous beams of the
nation's heart, as black cotton
absorbs the heat of the sun and holds it. There is
no way to know how easy this
white skin makes my life, this
life he could break so easily, the way I
think his own back is being broken, the
rod of his soul that at birth was dark and

fluid, rich as the heart of a seedling
ready to thrust up into any available light.

The Food-Thief

(Uganda, drought)

They drive him along the road in the steady
conscious way they drove their cattle
when they had cattle, when they had homes and
living children. They drive him with pliant
peeled sticks, snapped from trees
whose bark cannot be eaten—snapped,
not cut, no one has a knife, and the trees that can be
eaten have been eaten leaf and trunk and the
roots pulled from the ground and eaten.
They drive him and beat him, a loose circle of
thin men with sapling sticks,
driving him along slowly, slowly
beating him to death. He turns to them
with all the eloquence of the body, the
wrist turned out and the vein up his forearm
running like a root just under the surface, the
wounds on his head ripe and wet as a
loam furrow cut back and cut back at
plough-time to farrow a trench for the seed, his
eye pleading, the white a dark
occluded white like cloud-cover on the
morning of a day of heavy rain.
His lips are open to his brothers as the body of a
woman might be open, as the earth itself was
split and folded back and wet and
seedy to them once, the lines on his lips
fine as the thousand tributaries of a
root-hair, a river, he is asking them for life
with his whole body, and they are driving his body
all the way down the road because
they know the life he is asking for—
it is their life.

The Girl

They chased her and her friend through the woods
and caught them in a waste clearing, broken
random bracken, a couple of old mattresses,
as if the place had been prepared.
The thin one with straight hair
started raping her best friend,
and the curly one stood above her,
thrust his thumbs back inside her jaws, she was twelve,
stuck his penis in her mouth and throat
faster and faster and faster.
Then the straight-haired one stood up—
they lay like pulled-up roots at his feet,
naked twelve-year-old girls—he said
Now you're going to know what it's like
to be shot five times and slaughtered like a pig,
and they switched mattresses,
the blond was raping and stabbing her friend,
the straight-haired one sticking inside her
in one place and then another,
the point of his gun pressed deep into her waist,
she felt a little click in her spine and a
sting like 7-Up in her head, and then he
pulled the tree-branch across her throat
and everything went dark,
the gym went dark, and her mother's kitchen,
even the globes of light on the rounded
lips of her mother's nesting bowls went dark.

When she woke up, she was lying on the cold
copper-smelling earth, the mattress was pulled up
over her like a blanket, she saw
the dead body of her best friend

and she began to run,
she came to the edge of the woods and she stepped
out from the trees, like a wound debriding,
she walked across the field to the tracks
and said to the railway brakeman *Please, sir. Please, sir.*

At the trial she had to say everything—
her elder sister helped her with the words—
she had to sit in the room with them
and point to them. Now she goes to parties
but does not smoke, she is a cheerleader,
she throws her body up in the air
and kicks her legs and comes home and does the dishes
and her homework, she has to work hard in math,
the sky over the roof of her bed
filled with white planets. Every night
she prays for the soul of her best friend and
then thanks God for life. She knows
what all of us want never to know
and she does a cartwheel, the splits, she shakes the
shredded pom-poms in her fists.

The Pope's Penis

It hangs deep in his robes, a delicate
clapper at the center of a bell.
It moves when he moves, a ghostly fish in a
halo of silver seaweed, the hair
swaying in the dimness and the heat—and at night,
while his eyes sleep, it stands up
in praise of God.

When

I wonder, now, only when it will happen,
when the young mother will hear the
noise like somebody's pressure cooker
down the block, going off. She'll go out in the yard,
holding her small daughter in her arms,
and there, above the end of the street, in the
air above the line of the trees,
she will see it rising, lifting up
over our horizon, the upper rim of the
gold ball, large as a giant
planet starting to lift up over ours.
She will stand there in the yard holding her daughter,
looking at it rise and glow and blossom and rise,
and the child will open her arms to it,
it will look so beautiful.

I Go Back to May 1937

I see them standing at the formal gates of their colleges,
I see my father strolling out
under the ochre sandstone arch, the
red tiles glinting like bent
plates of blood behind his head, I
see my mother with a few light books at her hip
standing at the pillar made of tiny bricks,
the wrought-iron gate still open behind her, its
sword-tips aglow in the May air,
they are about to graduate, they are about to get married,
they are kids, they are dumb, all they know is they are
innocent, they would never hurt anybody.
I want to go up to them and say Stop,
don't do it—she's the wrong woman,
he's the wrong man, you are going to do things
you cannot imagine you would ever do,
you are going to do bad things to children,
you are going to suffer in ways you have not heard of,
you are going to want to die. I want to go
up to them there in the late May sunlight and say it,
her hungry pretty face turning to me,
her pitiful beautiful untouched body,
his arrogant handsome face turning to me,
his pitiful beautiful untouched body,
but I don't do it. I want to live. I
take them up like the male and female
paper dolls and bang them together
at the hips, like chips of flint, as if to
strike sparks from them, I say
Do what you are going to do, and I will tell about it.

Alcatraz

When I was a girl, I knew I was a man
because they might send me to Alcatraz
and only men went to Alcatraz.
Every time we drove to the city,
I'd see it there, white as a white
shark in the shark-rich Bay, the bars like
milk-white ribs. I knew I had pushed my
parents too far, my inner badness had
spread like ink and taken me over, I could
not control my terrible thoughts,
terrible looks, and they had often said
they would send me there—maybe the very next
time I spilled my milk, *Ala
Cazam*, the aluminum doors would slam, I'd be
there where I belonged, a girl-faced man in the
prison no one had escaped from. I did not
fear the other prisoners,
I knew who they were, men like me who had
spilled their milk one time too many,
not been able to curb their thoughts—
what I feared was the horror of the circles: circle of
sky around the earth, circle of
land around the Bay, circle of
water around the island, circle of
sharks around the shore, circle of
outer walls, inner walls,
steel girders, chrome bars,
circle of my cell around me, and there at the
center, the glass of milk and the guard's
eyes upon me as I reached out for it.

Why My Mother Made Me

Maybe I am what she always wanted,
my father as a woman,
maybe I am what she wanted to be
when she first saw him, tall and smart,
standing there in the college yard with the
hard male light of 1937
shining on his slicked hair. She wanted that
power. She wanted that size. She pulled and
pulled through him as if he were silky
bourbon taffy, she pulled and pulled and
pulled through his body till she drew me out,
sticky and gleaming, her life after her life.
Maybe I am the way I am
because she wanted exactly that,
wanted there to be a woman
a lot like her, but who would not hold back, so she
pressed herself, hard, against him,
pressed and pressed the clear soft
ball of herself like a stick of beaten cream
against his stained sour steel grater
until I came out the other side of his body,
a tall woman, stained, sour, sharp,
but with that milk at the center of my nature.
I lie here now as I once lay
in the crook of her arm, her creature,
and I feel her looking down into me the way
the maker of a sword gazes at his face
in the steel of the blade.

After 37 Years My Mother
Apologizes for My Childhood

When you tilted toward me, arms out
like someone trying to walk through a fire,
when you swayed toward me, crying out you were
sorry for what you had done to me, your
eyes filling with terrible liquid like
balls of mercury from a broken thermometer
skidding on the floor, when you quietly screamed
Where else could I turn? Who else did I have?, the
chopped crockery of your hands swinging toward me, the
water cracking from your eyes like moisture from
stones under heavy pressure, I could not
see what I would do with the rest of my life.
The sky seemed to be splintering, like a window
someone is bursting into or out of, your
tiny face glittered as if with
shattered crystal, with true regret, the
regret of the body. I could not see what my
days would be, with you sorry, with
you wishing you had not done it, the
sky falling around me, its shards
glistening in my eyes, your old, soft
body fallen against me in horror I
took you in my arms, I said *It's all right,
don't cry, it's all right*, the air filled with
flying glass, I hardly knew what I
said or who I would be now that I had forgiven you.

Cambridge Elegy

(for Henry Averell Gerry, 1941–60)

I scarcely know how to speak to you now,
you are so young now, closer to my daughter's age
than mine—but I have been there and seen it, and must
tell you, as the seeing and hearing
spell the world into the deaf-mute's hand.
The dormer windows like the ears of a fox, like the
double row of teats on a pig, still
perk up over the Square, though they're digging up the
street now, as if digging a grave,
the shovels shrieking on stone like your car
sliding on its roof after the crash.
How I wanted everyone to die if you had to die,
how sealed into my own world I was,
deaf and blind. What can I tell you now,
now that I know so much and you are a
freshman, still, drinking a quart of orange juice and
playing three sets of tennis to cure a hangover, such an
ardent student of the grown-ups! I can tell you
we were right, our bodies were right, life was
really going to be that good, that
pleasurable in every cell.
Suddenly I remember the exact look of your body, but
better than the bright corners of your eyes, or the
light of your face, the rich Long Island
puppy-fat of your thighs, or the shined
chino of your pants bright in the corners of my eyes, I
remember your extraordinary act of courage in
loving me, something no one but the
blind and halt had done before. You were
fearless, you could drive after a sleepless night
just like a grown-up, and not be afraid, you could
fall asleep at the wheel easily and

never know it, each blond hair of your head—and they were
thickly laid—put out like a filament of light,
twenty years ago. The Charles still
slides by with that ease that made me bitter when I
wanted all things hard as your death was hard,
wanted all things broken and rigid as the
bricks in the sidewalk or your love for me
stopped cell by cell in your young body.
Ave—I went ahead and had the children,
the life of ease and faithfulness, the
palm and the breast, every millimeter of delight in the body,
I took the road we stood on at the start together, I
took it all without you as if
in taking it after all I could most
honor you.

Topography

After we flew across the country we
got in bed, laid our bodies
intricately together, like maps laid
face to face, East to West, my
San Francisco against your New York, your
Fire Island against my Sonoma, my
New Orleans deep in your Texas, your Idaho
bright on my Great Lakes, my Kansas
burning against your Kansas your Kansas
burning against my Kansas, your Eastern
Standard Time pressing into my
Pacific Time, my Mountain Time
beating against your Central Time, your
sun rising swiftly from the right my
sun rising swiftly from the left your
moon rising slowly from the left my
moon rising slowly from the right until
all four bodies of the sky
burn above us, sealing us together,
all our cities twin cities,
all our states united, one
nation, indivisible, with liberty and justice for all.

I Cannot Forget the Woman
in the Mirror

Backwards and upside down in the twilight, that
woman on all fours, her head
dangling, and suffused, her lean
haunches, the area of darkness, the flanks and
ass narrow and pale as a deer's and those
breasts hanging down toward the center of the earth like
        plummets, when I
swayed from side to side they swayed, it was
so near night I couldn't tell if they were yellow or
violet or rose. I cannot get over her
moving toward him upside down in the mirror like a
fly on the ceiling, her head hanging down and her
tongue long and purple as an anteater's
going toward his body, she was clearly a human
animal, like an Iroquois scout creeping
naked and noiseless, and when I looked at her
she looked at me so directly, her eyes all
pupil, her stare said to me I
belong here, this is mine, I am living out my
true life on this earth.

The Moment the Two Worlds Meet

That's the moment I always think of—when the
slick, whole body comes out of me,
when they pull it out, not pull it but steady it
as it pushes forth, not catch it but keep their
hands under it as it pulses out,
they are the first to touch it,
and it shines, it glistens with the thick liquid on it.
That's the moment, while it's sliding, the limbs
compressed close to the body, the arms
bent like a crab's cloud-muscle legs, the
thighs packed plums in heavy syrup, the
legs folded like the wings of a chicken—
that is the center of life, the moment when the
juiced, bluish sphere of the baby is
sliding between the two worlds,
wet, like sex, it *is* sex,
it is my life opening back and back
as you'd strip the reed from the bud, not strip it but
watch it thrust so it peels itself and the
flower is there, severely folded, and
then it begins to open and dry
but by then the moment is over,
they wipe off the grease and wrap the child in a blanket and
hand it to you entirely in this world.

Little Things

After she's gone to camp, in the early
evening I clear our girl's breakfast dishes
from the rosewood table, and find a dinky
crystallized pool of maple syrup, the
grains standing there, round, in the night, I
rub it with my fingertip
as if I could read it, this raised dot of
amber sugar, and this time,
when I think of my father, I wonder why
I think of my father, of the Vulcan blood-red
glass in his hand, or his black hair gleaming like a
broken-open coal. I think I learned
to love the little things about him
because of all the big things
I could not love, no one could, it would be wrong to.
So when I fix on this image of resin,
or sweep together with the heel of my hand a
pile of my son's sunburn peels like
insect wings, where I peeled his back the night before camp,
I am doing something I learned early to do, I am
paying attention to small beauties,
whatever I have—as if it were our duty
to find things to love, to bind ourselves to this world.

The Month of June: 13½

As our daughter approaches graduation and
puberty at the same time, at her
own, calm, deliberate, serious rate,
she begins to kick up her heels, jazz out her
hands, thrust out her hipbones, chant
I'm great! I'm great! She feels 8th grade coming
open around her, a chrysalis cracking and
letting her out, it falls behind her and
joins the other husks on the ground,
7th grade, 6th grade, the
magenta rind of 5th grade, the
hard jacket of 4th when she had so much pain,
3rd grade, 2nd, the dim cocoon of
1st grade back there somewhere on the path, and
kindergarten like a strip of thumb-suck blanket
taken from the actual blanket they wrapped her in at birth.
The whole school is coming off her shoulders like a
cloak unclasped, and she dances forth in her
jerky sexy child's joke dance of
self, self, her throat tight and a
hard new song coming out of it, while her
two dark eyes shine
above her body like a good mother and a
good father who look down and
love everything their baby does, the way she
lives their love.

Looking at Them Asleep

When I come home late at night and go in to kiss them,
I see my girl with her arm curled around her head,
her mouth a little puffed, like one sated, but
slightly pouted like one who hasn't had enough,
her eyes so closed you would think they have rolled the
iris around to face the back of her head,
the eyeball marble-naked under that
thick satisfied desiring lid,
she lies on her back in abandon and sealed completion,
and the son in his room, oh the son he is sideways in his bed,
one knee up as if he is climbing
sharp stairs, up into the night,
and under his thin quivering eyelids you
know his eyes are wide open and
staring and glazed, the blue in them so
anxious and crystally in all this darkness, and his
mouth is open, he is breathing hard from the climb
and panting a bit, his brow is crumpled
and pale, his fine fingers curved,
his hand open, and in the center of each hand
the dry dirty boyish palm
resting like a cookie. I look at him in his
quest, the thin muscles of his arms
passionate and tense, I look at her with her
face like the face of a snake who has swallowed a deer,
content, content—and I know if I wake her she'll
smile and turn her face toward me though
half asleep and open her eyes and I
know if I wake him he'll jerk and say Don't and sit
up and stare about him in blue
unrecognition, oh my Lord how I
know these two. When love comes to me and says
What do you know, I say This girl, this boy.

from *The Father*

The Glass

I think of it with wonder now,
the glass of mucus that stood on the table
in front of my father all weekend. The tumor
is growing fast in his throat these days,
and as it grows it sends out pus
like the sun sending out flares, those pouring
tongues. So my father has to gargle, cough,
spit a mouthful of thick stuff
into the glass every ten minutes or so,
scraping the rim up his lower lip
to get the last bit off his skin, then he
sets the glass down, on the table, and it
sits there, like a glass of beer foam,
shiny and faintly yellow, he gargles and
coughs and reaches for it again,
and gets the heavy sputum out,
full of bubbles and moving around like yeast—
he is like a god producing food from his own mouth.
He himself can eat nothing, anymore,
just a swallow of milk, sometimes,
cut with water, and even then
it cannot, always, get past the tumor,
and the next time the saliva comes up
it is ropey, he has to roll it in his throat
a minute to form it and get it up and dis-
gorge the oval globule into the
glass of phlegm, which stood there all day and
filled slowly with compound globes and I would
empty it, and it would fill again,
and shimmer there on the table until
the room seemed to turn around it
in an orderly way, a model of the solar system

turning around the sun,
my father the old earth that used to
lie at the center of the universe, now
turning with the rest of us
around his death, luminous glass of
spit on the table, these last mouthfuls of his life.

His Stillness

The doctor said to my father, "You asked me
to tell you when nothing more could be done.
That's what I'm telling you now." My father
sat quite still, as he always did,
especially not moving his eyes. I had thought
he would rave if he understood he would die,
wave his arms and cry out. He sat up,
thin, and clean, in his clean gown,
like a holy man. The doctor said,
"There are things we can do which might give you time,
but we cannot cure you." My father said,
"Thank you." And he sat, motionless, alone,
with the dignity of a foreign leader.
I sat beside him. This was my father.
He had known he was mortal. I had feared they would have to
tie him down. I had not remembered
he had always held still and kept quiet to bear things,
the liquor a way to keep still. I had not
known him. My father had dignity. At the
end of his life his life began
to wake in me.

The Lifting

Suddenly my father lifted up his nightie, I
turned my head away but he cried out
Share!, my nickname, so I turned and looked.
He was sitting in the high cranked-up bed with the
gown up, around his neck,
to show me the weight he had lost. I looked
where his solid ruddy stomach had been
and I saw the skin fallen into loose
soft hairy rippled folds
lying in a pool of folds
down at the base of his abdomen,
the gaunt torso of a big man
who will die soon. Right away
I saw how much his hips are like mine,
the lengthened, white angles, and then
how much his pelvis is shaped like my daughter's,
a chambered whelk-shell hollowed out,
I saw the folds of skin like something
poured, a thick batter, I saw
his rueful smile, the cast-up eyes as he
shows me his old body, he knows
I will be interested, he knows I will find him
appealing. If anyone had ever told me
I would sit by him and he'd pull up his nightie
and I'd look at his naked body, at the thick
bud of his glans, his penis in all that
sparse hair, look at him
in affection and uneasy wonder
I would not have believed it. But now I can still
see the tiny snowflakes, white and
night-blue, on the cotton of the gown as it
rises the way we were promised at death it would rise,
the veils would fall from our eyes, we would know everything.

The Race

When I got to the airport I rushed up to the desk,
bought a ticket, ten minutes later
they told me the flight was cancelled, the doctors
had said my father would not live through the night
and the flight was cancelled. A young man
with a dark brown moustache told me
another airline had a nonstop
leaving in seven minutes. See that
elevator over there, well go
down to the first floor, make a right, you'll
see a yellow bus, get off at the
second Pan Am terminal, I
ran, I who have no sense of direction
raced exactly where he'd told me, a fish
slipping upstream deftly against
the flow of the river. I jumped off that bus with those
bags I had thrown everything into
in five minutes, and ran, the bags
wagged me from side to side as if
to prove I was under the claims of the material,
I ran up to a man with a flower on his breast,
I who always go to the end of the line, I said
Help me. He looked at my ticket, he said
Make a left and then a right, go up the moving stairs and then
run. I lumbered up the moving stairs,
at the top I saw the corridor,
and then I took a deep breath, I said
Goodbye to my body, goodbye to comfort,
I used my legs and heart as if I would
gladly use them up for this,
to touch him again in this life. I ran, and the
bags banged against me, wheeled and coursed

in skewed orbits, I have seen pictures of
women running, their belongings tied
in scarves grasped in their fists, I blessed my
long legs he gave me, my strong
heart I abandoned to its own purpose,
I ran to Gate 17 and they were
just lifting the thick white
lozenge of the door to fit it into
the socket of the plane. Like the one who is not
too rich, I turned sideways and
slipped through the needle's eye, and then
I walked down the aisle toward my father. The jet
was full, and people's hair was shining, they were
smiling, the interior of the plane was filled with a
mist of gold endorphin light,
I wept as people weep when they enter heaven,
in massive relief. We lifted up
gently from one tip of the continent
and did not stop until we set down lightly on the
other edge, I walked into his room
and watched his chest rise slowly
and sink again, all night
I watched him breathe.

Wonder

When she calls to tell me my father is dying
today or tomorrow, I walk down the hall
and feel that my mouth has fallen open
and my eyes are staring. The planet of his head
swam above my crib, I did not understand it.
His body came toward me in the lake over the agates,
the hair of his chest lifting like root-hairs—
I saw it and I did not understand it.
He lay, behind beveled-glass doors, beside
the cut-crystal decanter, its future
shards in upright bound sheaves.
He sat by his pool, not meeting our eyes,
his irises made of some boiled-down, viscous
satiny matter, undiscovered.
When he sickened, he began to turn to us,
when he sank down, he shined. I lowered my
mouth to the glistening tureen of his face
and he tilted himself toward me, a dazzling
meteor dropping down into the crib,
and now he is going to die. I walk down the
hall, face to face with it,
as if it were a great heat.
I feel like one of the shepherd children
when the star came down onto the roof.
But I am used to it, I stand in familiar
astonishment. If I had dared to imagine
trading, I might have wished to trade
places with anyone raised on love,
but how would anyone raised on love
bear this death?

The Feelings

When the intern listened to the stopped heart
I stared at him, as if he or I
were wild, were from some other world, I had
lost the language of gestures, I could not
know what it meant for a stranger to push
the gown up along the body of my father.
My face was wet, my father's face
was faintly moist with the sweat of his life,
the last moments of hard work.
I was leaning against the wall, in the corner, and
he lay on the bed, we were both doing something,
and everyone else in the room believed in the Christian God,
they called my father *the shell on the bed*, I was the
only one there who knew
he was entirely gone, the only one
there to say goodbye to his body
that was all he was, I held, hard,
to his foot, I thought of the Inuit elder
holding the stern of the death canoe, I
let him out slowly into the physical world.
I felt the dryness of his lips under
my lips, I felt how even my slight
kiss moved his head on the pillow
the way things move as if on their own in shallow water,
I felt his hair rush through my fingers
like a wolf's, the walls shifted, the floor, the
ceiling wheeled as if I was not
walking out of the room but the room was
backing away around me. I would have
liked to stay beside him, ride by his
shoulder while they drove him to the place where they would
      burn him,

see him safely into the fire,
touch his ashes in their warmth, and bring my
finger to my tongue. The next morning,
I felt my husband's body on me
crushing me sweetly like a weight laid heavy on some
soft thing, some fruit, holding me
hard to this world. Yes the tears came
out like juice and sugar from the fruit—
the skin thins, and breaks, and rips, there are
laws on this earth, and we live by them.

His Ashes

The urn was heavy, small but so heavy,
like the time, weeks before he died,
when he needed to stand, I got my shoulder
under his armpit, my cheek against his
naked freckled warm back
while she held the urinal for him—he had
lost half his body weight
and yet he was so heavy we could hardly hold him up
while he got the fluid out, crackling and
sputtering like a wet fire. The urn had that
six-foot heaviness, it began
to warm in my hands as I held it, under
the blue fir tree, stroking it.
The shovel got the last earth
out of the grave—it must have made that
kind of gritty iron noise when they
scraped his ashes out of the grate—
the others would be here any minute and I
wanted to open the urn as if then
I would finally know him. On the wet lawn,
under the cones cloaked in their rosin, I
worked at the top, it gave and slipped off and
there it was, the actual matter of his being:
small, speckled lumps of bone
like eggs; a discolored curve of bone like a
fungus grown around a branch;
spotted pebbles—and the spots were the channels of his marrow
where the live orbs of the molecules
swam as if by their own strong will
and in each cell the chromosomes
tensed and flashed, tore themselves
away from themselves, leaving their shining

duplicates. I looked at the jumble
of shards like a crushed paper-wasp hive:
was that a bone of his wrist, was that from the
elegant knee he bent, was that
his jaw, was that from his skull that at birth was
flexible yet—I looked at him,
bone and the ash it lay in, chromium-
white as the shimmering coils of dust
the earth leaves behind it, as it rolls, you can
hear its heavy roaring as it rolls away.

Beyond Harm

A week after my father died
suddenly I understood
his fondness for me was safe—nothing
could touch it. In those last months,
his face would sometimes brighten when I would
enter the room, and his wife said
that once, when he was half asleep,
he smiled when she said my name. He respected
my spunk—when they tied me to the chair, that time,
they were tying up someone he respected, and when
he did not speak, for weeks, I was one of the
beings to whom he was not speaking,
someone with a place in his life. The last
week he even said it, once,
by mistake. I walked into his room, and said "How
are you," and he said, "I love you
too." From then on, I had
that word to lose. Right up to the last
moment, I could make some mistake, offend him, and with
one of his old mouths of disgust he could re-
skew my life. I did not think of it,
I was helping to take care of him,
wiping his face and watching him.
But then, a while after he died,
I suddenly thought, with amazement, he will always
love me now, and I laughed—he was dead, dead!

The Underlife

Waiting for the subway, looking down
into the pit where the train rides,
I see a section of grey rail de-
tach itself, and move along the packed
silt. It is the first rat I have seen
in years, at first I draw back, but then
I think of my son's mice and lean forward.
The rat is muscular, ash-grey,
silvery, filth-fluffy. You can see
light through the ears. It moves along the rail, it looks
cautious, domestic, innocent. Back
home, sitting on the bed, I see
a tawny lozenge in the sheet's pattern
begin to move, and of course it's a cockroach,
it has lived in all the other great cities
before their razing and after it.
Christ you guys, I address these creatures,
I know about the plates of the earth shifting
over the liquid core, I watched the
bourbon and then the cancer pull my
father under, I know all this. And the
roach and rat turn to me
with the swiveling turn of natural animals, and they
say to me We are not educators,
we come to you from him.

Natural History

When I think about eels, I think about Seattle,
the day I went back to my father's grave.
I knew we had buried ashes, a box
of oily fluff, and yet, as I approached,
it felt as if the length of him
were slung there, massive, slack,
a six-foot amber eel flung down
deep into the hill. The air was clammy,
greenish as the old Aquarium air when we
would enter from the Zoo. Whenever we saw
a carnivore, my father would offer
to feed me to it—tigers, crocodiles,
manta rays, and that lone moray
eel, it would ripple up to us, armless,
legless, lipless as a grin of terror.
How would you like a tasty girl, my
father would ask the eel, a minister
performing a marriage, *How would you like
to get in there with that*, he'd lift me up the
thick glass, as if I were rising
on the power of my own scream. Later I would
pass the living room, and see him
asleep, passed out, undulant, lax,
indifferent. And at his grave
it was much like that—
the glossy stone, below it the mashed
bouquet of ashes, and under that,
like a boy who has thrown himself down to cry, the
great, easy, stopped curve
of my father. Length to length I lay on it,
and slept.

The Ferryer

Three years after my father's death
he goes back to work. Unemployed
for twenty-five years, he's very glad
to be taken on again, shows up
on time, tireless worker. He sits
in the prow of the boat, sweet cox, turned
with his back to the carried. He is dead, but able
to kneel upright, facing forward
toward the other shore. Someone has closed
his mouth, so he looks more comfortable, not
thirsty or calling out, and his eyes
are open—under the iris, the black
line that appeared there in death. He is calm,
he is happy to be hired, he's in business again,
his new job is a joke between us and he
loves to have a joke with me, he keeps
a straight face. He waits, naked,
ivory bow figurehead,
ribs, nipples, lips, a gaunt
tall man, and when I bring people
and set them in the boat and push them off
my father poles them across the river
to the far bank. We don't speak,
he knows that this is simply someone
I want to get rid of, who makes me feel
ugly and afraid. I do not say
the way you did. He knows the labor
and loves it. When I dump someone in, he
does not look back, he takes them straight
to hell. He wants to work for me
until I die. Then, he knows, I will
come to him, get in his boat

and be taken across, then hold out my broad
hand to his, help him ashore, we will
embrace like two who were never born,
naked, not breathing, then up to our chins we will
pull the home blanket of earth and
rest together, at the end of the working day.

I Wanted to Be There When My Father Died

I wanted to be there when my father died
because I wanted to see him die—
and not just to know him, down
to the ground, the dirt of his unmaking, and not
just to give him a last chance
to give me something, or take his old loathing
back. All summer he had gagged, as if trying
to cough his whole esophagus out,
surely his pain and sorrow had appeased me,
and yet I wanted to see him die
not just to see no soul come
free of his body, no mucal genie of
spirit jump
forth from his mouth,
proving the body on earth is all we have got,
I wanted to watch my father die
because I hated him. Oh, I loved him,
my hands cherished him, laying him out,
but I had feared him so, his lying as if dead on the
couch had seemed to pummel me, an Eve
he took and pressed back into clay,
casual thumbs undoing the cheekbone
eye-socket rib pelvis ankle of the child
and now I watched him be undone and
someone in me gloried in it,
someone lying where he'd lain in chintz
Eden, some corpse girl, corkscrewed like
one of his bourbon spit-ems, smiled.
The priest was well called to that room,
violet grosgrain river of his ribbon laid
down well on that bank of flesh
where the daughter of death was made, it was well to say

Into other hands than ours
we commend this spirit.

Waste Sonata

I think at some point I looked at my father
and thought *He's full of shit.* How did I
know fathers talked to their children,
kissed them? I knew. I saw him and judged him.
Whatever he poured into my mother
she hated, her face rippled like a thin
wing, sometimes, when she happened to be near him,
and the liquor he knocked into his body
felled him, slew the living tree,
loops of its grain started to cube,
petrify, coprofy, he was a
shit, but I felt he hated being a shit,
he had never imagined it could happen, this drunken
sleep was a spell laid on him—
by my mother. Well, I left to them
the passion of who did what to whom, it was a
baby in their bed they were rolling over on,
but I could not live with hating him.
I did not see that I had to. I stood
in that living room and saw him drowse
like the prince, in slobbrous beauty, I began
to think he was a kind of chalice,
a grail, his love the goal of a quest,
yes! He was the god of love
and I was a shit. I looked down at my forearm—
whatever was inside there
was not good, it was white stink,
bad manna. I looked in the mirror, and
as I looked at my face the blemishes
arose, like pigs up out of the ground
to the witch's call. It was strange to me
that my body smelled sweet, it was proof I was

demonic, but at least I breathed out,
from the sour dazed scum within,
my father's truth. Well it's fun talking about this,
I love the terms of foulness. I have learned
to get some pleasure from speaking of pain.
But to die, like this. To grow old and die
a child, lying to herself.
My father was not a shit. He was a man
failing at life. He had little shits
traveling through him while he lay there unconscious—
sometimes I don't let myself say
I loved him, anymore, but I feel
I almost love those shits that move through him,
shapely, those waste foetuses,
my mother, my sister, my brother, and me
in that purgatory.

My Father Speaks to Me from the Dead

I seem to have woken up in a pot-shed,
on clay, on shards, the glitter paths
of slugs kiss-crossing my body. I don't know
where to start, with this grime on me.
I take the spider glue-net, plug
of the dead, out of my mouth, let's see
if where I have been I can do this.
I love your feet. I love your knees,
I love your our my legs, they are so
long because they are yours and mine
both. I love your—what can I call it,
between your legs, we never named it, the
glint and purity of its curls. I love
your rear end, I changed you once,
washed the detritus off your tiny
bottom, with my finger rubbed
the oil on you; when I touched your little
anus I crossed wires with God for a moment.
I never hated your shit—that was
your mother. I love your navel, thistle
seed fossil, even though
it's her print on you. Of course I love
your breasts—did you see me looking up
from within your daughter's face, as she nursed?
I love your bony shoulders and you know I
love your hair, thick and live
as earth. And I never hated your face,
I hated its eruptions. You know what I love?
I love your brain, its halves and silvery
folds, like a woman's labia.
I love in you
even what comes

from deep in your mother—your heart, that hard worker,
and your womb, it is a heaven to me,
I lie on its gentle hills and gaze up
at its rosy vault.
I have been in a body without breath,
I have been in the morgue, in fire, in the slagged
chimney, in the air over the earth,
and buried in the earth, and pulled down
into the ocean—where I have been
I understand this life, I am matter,
your father, I made you, when I say now that I love you
I mean look down at your hand, move it,
that action is matter's love, for human
love go elsewhere.

from *The Wellspring*

My Parents' Wedding Night, 1937

Today, I thought of that blood, rippling out
like the blood that seeps up out of the side
of a trout when the pressed-down blade breaks through,
tough salty sweet fish
of my mother's maidenhead. It was in the dark,
the harsh shantung blinds drawn down, the
ruffled curtains unloosed at the waist.
She was naked with a man for the first time,
the intricate embroidery silks of her
pudenda moist upright alert
terrified, thrilled, each hair
reaching out and curling back, she was
there in the bed like her own parents,
there at the center of the world. Now
she was the loaf laid into the pan
raw and being fed now into the bright oven.
And I thought of my father, over her,
ivory-white face and brilliantine hair,
up on his elbows like a man pulling himself
out of the ocean onto the beach. The war
had not yet begun, they lay and slept
in blood and peace, no one knew what was coming.

I leave them wrapped in that sheet, double larvum,
they sleep with their mouths open like teenagers
in the smell of champagne and cruor and semen,
they rest but I go back and back to that moment,
looking at it until I get more used to it,
like my childhood God watching Adam and Eve in the garden—
the first springing wrinkle of blood, I
see it as a castaway sees the leap of
life pouring out of the turtle's throat where the shell severs it.

Japanese-American Farmhouse,
California, 1942

Everything has been stolen that anyone
thought worth stealing. The stairs into the grass
are scattered with sycamore leaves curled
like ammonites in inland rock.
Wood shows through the paint on the frame
and the door is open—an empty room,
sunlight on the floor. All that is left
on the porch is the hollow cylinder
of an Alber's Quick Oats cardboard box
and a sewing machine. Its extraterrestrial
head is bowed, its scrolled neck
glistens. I was born, that day, near there,
in wartime, of ignorant people.

Killing My Sister's Fish

I picked up the bottle with its gladiator shoulders—
inside its shirred greyish plastic
the ammonia, more muscular than water, pungent—
I poured one dollop, gleaming genie,
into the bowl with my sister's goldfish
just because they were alive, and she liked them.
It was in the basement, near the zinc-lined sinks
and the ironing board, next to the boiler,
beside the door to the cellar from which
I could get into the crawl space
under the corner of the house, and lie
on the dirt on my back, as if passed out.
I may have been on my way there
when I saw the bowl, and the ammonia curled
for a moment in the air like a spirit. Then I crawled up
under the floor-joists, into the tangent
where the soil curved up, and I lay there,
at the ends of the earth, as if without
regret, as if something set in motion
long before I had been conceived
had been accomplished.

Mrs. Krikorian

She saved me. When I arrived in 6th grade,
a known criminal, the new teacher
asked me to stay after school the first day, she said
I've heard about you. She was a tall woman,
with a deep crevice between her breasts,
and a large, calm nose. She said,
This is a special library pass.
As soon as you finish your hour's work—
that hour's work that took ten minutes
and then the devil glanced into the room
and found me empty, a house standing open—
you can go to the library. Every hour
I'd zip through the work in a dash and slip out of my
seat as if out of God's side and sail
down to the library, solo through the empty
powerful halls, flash my pass
and stroll over to the dictionary
to look up the most interesting word
I knew, *spank*, dipping two fingers
into the jar of library paste to
suck that tart mucilage as I
came to the page with the cocker spaniel's
silks curling up like the fine steam of the body.
After *spank*, and *breast*, I'd move on
to *Abe Lincoln* and *Helen Keller*,
safe in their goodness till the bell, thanks
to Mrs. Krikorian, amiable giantess
with the kind eyes. When she asked me to write
a play, and direct it, and it was a flop, and I
hid in the coat-closet, she brought me a candy-cane
as you lay a peppermint on the tongue, and the worm
will come up out of the bowel to get it.

And so I was emptied of Lucifer
and filled with school glue and eros and
Amelia Earhart, saved by Mrs. Krikorian.
And who had saved Mrs. Krikorian?
When the Turks came across Armenia, who
slid her into the belly of a quilt, who
locked her in a chest, who mailed her to America?
And *that* one, who saved *her*, and *that* one—
who saved *her*, to save the one
who saved Mrs. Krikorian, who was
standing there on the sill of 6th grade, a
wide-hipped angel, smokey hair
standing up weightless all around her head?
I end up owing my soul to so many,
to the Armenian nation, one more soul someone
jammed behind a stove, drove
deep into a crack in a wall,
shoved under a bed. I would wake
up, in the morning, under my bed—not
knowing how I had got there—and lie
in the dusk, the dustballs beside my face
round and ashen, shining slightly
with the eerie comfort of what is neither good nor evil.

First

He stood in the sulphur baths, his calves
against the stone rim of the pool
where his half-full glass of scotch stood, his
shins wavering in the water, his torso
looming over me, huge, in the night,
a grown-up man's body, softer and
warmer with the clothes off—I was a sophomore
at college, in the baths with a naked man,
a writer, married, a father, widowed,
remarried, separated, unreadable, and when I
said No, I was sorry, I couldn't,
he'd invented this, rising and dripping
in the heavy sodium water, giving me
his body to suck. I had not heard
of this, I was moved by his innocence and daring,
I went to him like a baby who's been crying
for hours for milk. He stood and moaned
and rocked his knees, I felt I knew
what his body wanted me to do, like rubbing
my mother's back, receiving directions
from her want into the nerves of my hands.
In the smell of the trees of seaweed rooted in
ocean trenches just offshore,
and the mineral liquid from inside the mountain,
I gave over to flesh like church music
until he drew out and held himself and
something flew past me like a fresh ghost.
We sank into the water and lay there, napes
on the rim. *I've never done that before,*
I said. His eyes not visible
to me, his voice muffled, he said, *You've been
sucking cock since you were fourteen,*

and fell asleep. I stayed beside him
so he wouldn't go under, he snored like my father, I
tried not to think about what he had said,
but then I saw, in it, the unmeant
gift—that I was good at this
raw mystery I liked. I sat
and rocked, by myself, in the fog, in the smell
of kelp, night steam like animals' breath,
there where the harsh granite and quartz dropped down
into and under the start of the western sea.

Adolescence

When I think of my adolescence, I think
of the bathroom of that seedy hotel
in San Francisco, where my boyfriend would take me.
I had never seen a bathroom like that—
no curtains, no towels, no mirror, just
a sink green with grime and a toilet
yellow and rust-colored—like something in a science experiment,
growing the plague in bowls.
Sex was still a crime, then,
I'd sign out of my college dorm
to a false destination, sign into
the flophouse under a false name,
go down the hall to the one bathroom
and lock myself in. And I could not learn to get that
diaphragm in, I'd decorate it
like a cake, with glistening spermicide,
and lean over, and it would leap from my fingers
and sail, into a corner, to land
in a concave depression like a rat's nest,
I'd bend and pluck it out and wash it
and wash it down to that fragile dome,
I'd frost it again till it was shimmering
and bend it into its tensile arc and it would
fly through the air, rim humming
like Saturn's ring, I would bow down and crawl to retrieve it.
When I think of being eighteen,
that's what I see, that brimmed disc
floating through the air and descending, I see myself
kneeling and reaching, reaching for my own life.

May 1968

When the Dean said we could not cross campus
until the students gave up the buildings,
we lay down in the street,
we said the cops will enter this gate
over us. Lying back on the cobbles,
I saw the buildings of New York City
from dirt level, they soared up
and stopped, chopped off—above them, the sky,
the night air, over the island.
The mounted police moved, near us,
while we sang, and then I began to count,
12, 13, 14, 15
I counted again, 15, 16, one
month since the day on that deserted beach,
17, 18, my mouth fell open,
my hair on the street,
if my period did not come tonight
I was pregnant. I could see the sole of a cop's
shoe, the gelding's belly, its genitals—
if they took me to Women's Detention and did
the exam on me, the speculum,
the fingers—I gazed into the horse's tail
like a comet-train. I'd been thinking I might
get arrested, I had been half wanting
to give myself away. On the tar—
one brain in my head, another
in the making, near the base of my tail—
I looked at the steel arc of the horse's
shoe, the curve of its belly, the cop's
nightstick, the buildings streaming up
away from the earth. I knew I should get up
and leave, but I lay there looking at the space

above us, until it turned deep blue and then
ashy, colorless, *Give me this one
night,* I thought, *and I'll give this child
the rest of my life,* the horses' heads,
this time, drooping, dipping, until
they slept in a circle around my body and my daughter.

Bathing the New Born

I love with an almost fearful love
to remember the first baths I gave him,
our second child, so I knew what to do,
I laid the little torso along
my left forearm, nape of the neck
in the crook of my elbow, hips nearly as
small as a least tern's tail
against my wrist, thigh held loosely
in the loop of thumb and forefinger, the
sign that means exactly right. I'd soap him,
the violet, cold feet, the scrotum
wrinkled as a waved whelk, the chest,
hands, clavicles, throat, gummy
furze of the scalp. When I got him too soapy he'd
slide in my grip like an armful of buttered
noodles, but I'd hold him not too tight,
I felt that I was good for him,
I'd tell him about his wonderful body
and the wonderful soap, and he'd look up at me,
one week old, his eyes still wide
and apprehensive. I love that time
when you croon and croon to them, you can see
the calm slowly entering them, you can
sense it in your clasping hand,
the loose spine relaxing against
the muscle of your forearm, you feel the fear
leaving their bodies, he lay in the blue
oval plastic baby tub and
looked at me in wonder and began to
move his silky limbs at will in the water.

41, Alone, No Gerbil

In the strange quiet, I realize
there's no one else in the house. No bucktooth
mouth pulls at a stainless-steel teat, no
hairy mammal runs on a treadmill—
Charlie is dead, the last of our children's half-children.
When our daughter found him lying in the shavings, trans-
mogrified backwards from a living body
into a bolt of rodent bread
she turned her back on early motherhood
and went on single, with nothing. Crackers,
Fluffy, Pretzel, Biscuit, Charlie,
buried on the old farm we bought
where she could know nature. Well, now she knows it
and it sucks. Creatures she loved, mobile and
needy, have gone down stiff and indifferent,
she will not adopt again though she cannot
have children yet, her body is like
a blueprint for a woman's body,
so now everything stops, for a while,
now I must wait many years
to hear in this house again the faint
powerful call of a young animal.

Physics

Her first puzzle had three pieces,
she'd take the last piece, and turn it,
and lower it in, like a sewer-lid,
flush with the street. The bases of the frames were like
wooden fur, guard-hairs sticking out
of the pelt. I'd set one on the floor and spread
the pieces out around it. It makes me
groan to think of Red Riding Hood's hood,
a single, scarlet, pointed piece, how
long since I have seen her. Later, panthers,
500 pieces, and an Annunciation,
1000 pieces, we would gaze, on our elbows,
into its gaps. Now she tells me
that if I were sitting in a twenty-foot barn,
with the doors open at either end,
and a fifty-foot ladder hurtled through the barn
at the speed of light, there would be a moment
—after the last rung was inside the barn
and before the first rung came out the other end—
when the whole fifty-foot ladder would be
inside the twenty-foot barn, and I believe her,
I have thought her life was inside my life
like that. When she reads the college catalogues, I
look away and hum. I have not grown
up yet, I have lived as my daughter's mother
the way I had lived as my mother's daughter,
inside her life. I have not been born yet.

My Son the Man

Suddenly his shoulders get a lot wider,
the way Houdini would expand his body
while people were putting him in chains. It seems
no time since I would help him put on his sleeper,
guide his calves into the shadowy interior,
zip him up and toss him up and
catch his weight. I cannot imagine him
no longer a child, and I know I must get ready,
get over my fear of men now my son
is going to be one. This was not
what I had in mind when he pressed up through me like a
sealed trunk through the ice of the Hudson,
snapped the padlock, unsnaked the chains,
appeared in my arms. Now he looks at me
the way Houdini studied a box
to learn the way out, then smiled and let himself be manacled.

First Formal

She rises up above the strapless, her dewy
flesh like a soul half out of a body.
It makes me remember her one week old,
mollescent, elegant, startled, alone.
She stands quite still, as if, if she moved,
her body might pour up out of the bodice,
she keeps her steady gaze raised
when she walks, she looks exactly forward,
led by some radar of the strapless, or with
a cup runneth over held perfectly level, her
almost seasick beauty shimmering
a little. She looks brave, shoulders
made of some extra-visible element,
or as if some of her cells, tonight,
were faceted like a fly's eye, and her
skin was seeing us see it. She looks
hatched this moment, and yet weary—she would lie
in her crib, so slight, worn out from her journey,
and gaze at the world and at us in dubious willingness.

High School Senior

For seventeen years, her breath in the house
at night, puff, puff, like summer
cumulus above her bed,
and her scalp smelling of apricots
—this being who had formed within me,
squatted like a wide-eyed tree-frog in the night,
like an eohippus she had come out of history
slowly, through me, into the daylight,
I had the daily sight of her,
like food or air she was there, like a mother.
I say "college," but I feel as if I cannot tell
the difference between her leaving for college
and our parting forever—I try to see
this apartment without her, without her pure
depth of feeling, without her creek-brown
hair, her daedal hands with their tapered
fingers, her pupils brown as the mourning cloak's
wing, but I can't. Seventeen years
ago, in this room, she moved inside me,
I looked at the river, I could not imagine
my life with her. I gazed across the street,
and saw, in the icy winter sun,
a column of steam rush up away from the earth.
There are creatures whose children float away
at birth, and those who throat-feed their young for
weeks and never see them again. My daughter
is free and she is in me—no, my love
of her is in me, moving in my heart,
changing chambers, like something poured
from hand to hand, to be weighed and then reweighed.

The Pediatrician Retires

This is the archway where I stood, next to the
panel of frosted glass, when they told me
there was a chance it could be epilepsy, and
almost before my heart sank
I felt a new-made layer of something fold
over my will and wrap it, in an instant,
as if the body takes care of the parent
who takes care of the child. This is the door
we came through each week while the symptoms slowly
faded. That is the fruit-scale where she had
weighed him, and his arms had flown to the sides
in an infant Moro. And there are the chairs
where one sits with the infectious ones,
the three-year-olds calmly struggling for air, not
listless or scared, steady workers,
pulling breath through the constricted passage,
Yes, she says, *it's bronchial pneumonia*
and asthma, the same as last month, the parent's
heart suddenly stronger, like a muscle
the weight-lifter has worked. There is the room
where she took his blood and he watched the vial fill, he went
greener, and greener, and fainted, and she said,
Next time don't be brave, next time
shout! And here is the chair where I sat and she
said *If the nerve is dead, he will lose only*
partial use of the hand, and it's
the left hand—he's right-handed, isn't he?,
the girding, the triple binding of the heart.
This is the room where I sat, worried,
and opened the magazine, and saw
the war in Asia, a very young soldier
hanged by the neck—still a boy, almost,

not much older than the oldest children
in the waiting room. Suddenly its walls seemed
not quite real, as if we all
were in some large place together.
This is where I learned what I know,
the body university—
at graduation, we would cry, and throw
our ceiling-at-four-a.m. hats high in the air,
but I think that until the end of our life we are here.

This Hour

We could never really say what it is like,
this hour of drinking wine together
on a hot summer night, in the living room
with the windows open, in our underwear,
my pants with pale-gold gibbon monkeys on them
gleaming in the heat. We talk about our son disap-
pearing between the pine boughs,
we could not tell what was chrysalis or
bough and what was him. The wine
is powerful, each mouthful holds
for a moment its amber agate shape,
I think of the sweat I sipped from my father's
forehead the hour before his death. We talk about
those last days—that I was waiting for him to die.
You are lying on the couch, your underpants
a luminous white, your hand resting
relaxed, along the side of your penis,
we talk about your father's illness,
your nipple like a pure circle of
something risen to the surface of your chest.
Even if we wanted to,
we could not describe it,
the end of the second glass when I sometimes
weep and you start to get sleepy—I love
to drink and cry with you, and end up
sobbing to a sleeping man, your
long body filling the couch and
draped slightly over the ends, the
untrained soft singing of your snore, it cannot be given.
Yes, we know we will make love, but we're
not getting ready to make love,
nor are we getting over making love,

love is simply our element,
it is the summer night, we are in it.

Full Summer

I paused, and paused, over your body,
to feel the current of desire pull
and pull through me. Our hair was still wet,
mine like knotted wrack, it fell
across you as I paused, a soaked coil
around your glans. When one of your hairs
dried, it lifted like a bare nerve.
On the beach, above us, a cloud had appeared in
the clear air, a clockwise loop coming
in out of nothing, now the skin of your scrotum
moved like a live being, an animal,
I began to lick you, the foreskin lightly
stuck in one spot, like a petal, I love
to free it—just so—in joy,
and to sip from the little crying lips
at the tip. Then there was no more pausing,
nor was this the taker,
some new one came
and sucked, and up from where I had been hiding I was
drawn in a heavy spiral out of matter
over into another world
I had thought I would have to die to reach.

Am and Am Not

When I'm tilted forward, brushing my teeth,
I glance down. We do not know
ourselves. My cunt, like a hand, stroked him,
such subtle, intricate movement. Central
inside me this one I am and am not,
not only like a palm, more like a snake's
reticulated body, rings of muscle—
like the penis outside-in, its twin.
Who is it? I lean against the sink, mouth open
and burning with Colgate, nixie palate
scoured with pond-mint; is it my soul
in there, elastic as an early creature
gone out on its own again, is it my
soul's throat? Its rings ripple
in waves, as if it swallows, but what it
swallows stays, and grows, and grows,
we become one being, whom we hardly know,
whom we know better than we know anyone
else. And in the morning I look down. Who? What has—
what?! Seeing just the skin of the belly—
she is asleep in there, the soul, vertical
undulant one, she is dancing upright in her dream.

True Love

In the middle of the night, when we get up
after making love, we look at each other in
complete friendship, we know so fully
what the other has been doing. Bound to each other
like mountaineers coming down from a mountain,
bound with the tie of the delivery room,
we wander down the hall to the bathroom, I can
hardly walk, I wobble through the granular
shadowless air, I know where you are
with my eyes closed, we are bound to each other
with huge invisible threads, our sexes
muted, exhausted, crushed, the whole
body a sex—surely this
is the most blessed time of my life,
our children asleep in their beds, each fate
like a vein of abiding mineral
not discovered yet. I sit
on the toilet in the night, you are somewhere in the room,
I open the window and snow has fallen in a
steep drift, against the pane, I
look up, into it,
a wall of cold crystals, silent
and glistening, I quietly call to you
and you come and hold my hand and I say
I cannot see beyond it. I cannot see beyond it.

from *Blood, Tin, Straw*

The Promise

With the second drink, at the restaurant,
holding hands on the bare table,
we are at it again, renewing our promise
to kill each other. You are drinking gin,
night-blue juniper berry
dissolving in your body, I am drinking Fumé,
chewing its fragrant dirt and smoke, we are
taking on earth, we are part soil already,
and wherever we are, we are also in our
bed, fitted, naked, closely
along each other, half passed out,
after love, drifting back
and forth across the border of consciousness,
our bodies buoyant, clasped. Your hand
tightens on the table. You're a little afraid
I'll chicken out. What you do not want
is to lie in a hospital bed for a year
after a stroke, without being able
to think or die, you do not want
to be tied to a chair like your prim grandmother,
cursing. The room is dim around us,
ivory globes, pink curtains
bound at the waist—and outside,
a weightless, luminous, lifted-up
summer twilight. I tell you you do not
know me if you think I will not
kill you. Think how we have floated together
eye to eye, nipple to nipple,
sex to sex, the halves of a creature
drifting up to the lip of matter
and over it—you know me from the bright, blood-
flecked delivery room, if a lion

had you in its jaws I would attack it, if the ropes
binding your soul are your own wrists, I will cut them.

Know-Nothing

Sometimes I think I know nothing about sex.
All that I thought I was going to know,
that I did not know, I still do not know.
I think about this out of town,
on hotel elevators crowded with men.
The body of knowledge which lay somewhere
ahead of me, now I do not know where it
lies, or in the beds of strangers.
I know of sexual love, with my beloved,
but of men—I think there are women who know
men, I can't see what it is
they know, but I feel in myself that I
could know it, or could I have been a woman who
would dare that. I don't mean what she does
with herself, or that she would know more pleasure,
but she knows something true that I don't know,
she knows fucking with a stranger. I feel
in awe of that, why is she not
afraid, what if she did not like
his touch, or what he said, how
would she bear it? Or maybe she has mercy on pretty much
anything a stranger would say or do,
or maybe it is not mercy, but sex,
when she sees what he's like, she enflames for that,
and is afraid of nothing, wanting to touch
stone desire, and know it, she is like
a god, who could have sex with stranger
after stranger—she could know men.
But what of her womb, tender core
of her being, what of her breasts' stiff hearts,
and her dense eggs, what if she falls
in love? Maybe to know sex fully

one has to risk being destroyed by it.
Maybe only ruin could take
its full measure, as death stands
in the balance with birth, and ignorance with love.

Dear Heart,

How did you know to turn me over,
then, when I couldn't know to take
the moment to turn and start to begin
to finish, I was out there, far ahead
of my body, far ahead of the earth,
ahead of the moon—like someone on the other
side of the moon, stepped off, facing space, I was
floating out there, splayed, facing
away, fucked, fucked, my face
glistening and distorted pressed against the inner
caul of the world. I was almost beyond
pleasure, in a region of icy, absolute
sensing, my open mouth and love-slimed
cheeks stretching the membrane the way
the face of the almost born can appear, still
veiled in its casing, just inside
the oval portal, pausing, about
to split its glistering mask—you eased me
back, drew me back into the human
night, you turned me and the howling slowed, and at the
crux of our joining, flower heads grew
fast-motion against you, swelled and burst without
tearing—ruinless death, each
sepal, each petal, came to the naught
of earth, our portion, in ecstasy, ash
to fire to ash, dust to bloom to dust.

19

When we took the acid, his wife was off
with someone else, there was a hole in their bedroom
wall where the Steuben wedding owl
had flown from one room right through into another,
I was in love with his best friend, who had
gone into a monastery
after he'd deflowered me, so we
knew each other: when he finished, under
my palm, I could feel the circular ribs of his
penis; I finished with my legs wrapped around his
leg, even with my toes pointed, my
feet reached only halfway down
his calf, later I was lying on the bathroom
floor, looking up at him, naked, he was
6'6", a decathlete,
my eyes followed the inner line of his
leg, up, up, up,
up, up, up, up.
Weeks later, he would pull a wall-phone
out of a wall, he would cross the divider
in his Mustang at 2 a.m. with me and go
sixty, against traffic, crying, I could
hardly hear what he said about the barbed
wire and his father and his balls—but that
acid night, we stayed up all night, I was
not in love with him, so his beauty made me
happy, we chattered, we chatted naked, he
told me everything he liked
about my body—and he liked everything—
even the tiny gooseflesh bumps
around my hard nipples,
he said the way to make love to me

would be from behind, with that sheer angle, his
forefinger drew it, gently, the extreme
hairpin curve of the skinny buttocks,
he said it the way I thought an older
cousin in a dream might give advice
to a younger cousin, his fingertip
barely missing my—whatever, in love, one would
call the asshole—he regarded me with a
savoring kindness, from a cleft of sweet lust in the
human he actually looked at me
and thought how I best should be fucked. *Oooh.*
Oooh. It meant there was something to be done with me,
something exactly right, he looked at me
and saw it,
willing to not be the one
who did it—all night, he desired me and
protected me, he gazed at my body and un-
saw my parents' loathing, pore by
pore on my skin he closed that couple's eyes.

That Day

None of the pain was sharp. The sash
was pliant, its cotton blunt, like a bandage
it held my wrist to the chair. And the fierce
glazed string of the woven seat
printed me in deep pink, but I was
used to that, that matter could mark us
and its marks dissolve. That day, no one touched me,
it was a formal day, the nerves lay easy
in their planched grooves. The hunger grew, but
quietly, edgeless, a suckling in my stomach
doubling, it was a calm day
unfolding to its laws. Only the pleasure had been
sharp—the tilt of the squat bottle
over their bed, the way the ink
lowered itself, onto the spread, I had
felt its midnight, genie shape
leave my chest, pouring forth, and it was
India ink, the kind that does not come out,
I sat attached to the chair like Daphne
halfway out of the wood, and I read that blot.
I read it all day, like a Nancy Drew I was
in—they had said *You won't be fed
till you say you're sorry*, I was strangely happy, I would
never say I was sorry, I had left
that life behind. So it didn't surprise me when she
came in slowly, holding a bowl that
held what swayed and steamed, she sat and
spoon-fed me, in silence, hot
alphabet soup. Sharp pleasure
of my wing-tip hands hung down beside me
slack as I ate, sharp pleasure of the
legible school of edible letters flowed

in, over my taste-buds, B,
O, F, K, G,
I mashed the crescent moon of the C,
caressed the E, reading with my tongue
that boiled Braille—and she was almost kneeling to me
and I wasn't sorry. She was feeding the one
who wasn't sorry, the way you lay food
at the foot of an image. I sat there, tied,
taking in her offering
and wildly reading as I ate, S S F
T, L W B B P Q
B, she dipped into my mouth the mild
discordant fuel—she wanted me to thrive, and decipher.

After Punishment Was Done with Me

After punishment was done with me,
after I would put my clothes back on, I'd go
back to my room, close the door,
and wander around, ending up
on the floor sometimes, always, near the baseboard,
where the vertical fall of the wall meets
the level rule of the floor—I would put
my face near that angle, and look at the dust
and anything caught in the dust. I would see
the wedding swags of old-lady-hair—
pelmets carved on cenotaph granite—and
cocoons of slough like tiny Kotexes
wound and wound in toilet paper,
I would see the anonymous crowds of grit, as if
looking down into Piazza Navona
from a mile above Il Duce, I would see
a larval casing waisted in gold
thin as the poorest gold wedding band,
and a wasp's dried thorax and legs wound love-ring
with a pubic hair of my mother's, I would see
the coral-maroon of the ladybug's back
marked with its two, night genes,
I would see a fly curled up, dried,
its wings like the rabbit's ears, or the deer's.
I would lie quiet and look at them,
it was so peaceful there with them,
I was not at all afraid of them,
and my sadness for them didn't matter.
I would look at each piece of lint
and half imagine being it,
I would feel that I was looking at
the universe from a great distance.

Sometimes I'd pick up a Dresden fly
and gaze at it closely, sometimes I'd idly play
house with the miniature world, weddings and
funerals with barbed body parts,
awful births, but I did not want
to disarrange that unerring deadness
like a kind of goodness, corner of wetless
grey waste, nothing the human
would go for. Without desire or rage
I would watch that dust celestium as the pain
on my matter died and turned to spirit
and wandered the cloud world of home,
the ashes of the earth.

What Is the Earth?

The earth is a homeless person. Or
the earth's home is the atmosphere.
Or the atmosphere is the earth's clothing,
layers of it, the earth wears all of it,
the earth is a homeless person.
Or the atmosphere is the earth's cocoon,
which it spun itself, the earth is a larvum.
Or the atmosphere is the earth's skin—
earth, and atmosphere, one
homeless one. Or its orbit is the earth's
home, or the path of the orbit just
a path, the earth a homeless person.
Or the gutter of the earth's orbit is a circle
of hell, the circle of the homeless. But the earth
has a place, around the fire, the hearth
of our star, the earth is at home, the earth
is home to the homeless. For food, and warmth,
and shelter, and health, they have earth and fire
and air and water, for home they have
the elements they are made of, as if
each homeless one were an earth, made
of milk and grain, like Ceres, and one
could eat oneself—as if the human
were a god, who could eat the earth, a god
of homelessness.

Leaving the Island

On the ferry, on the last morning of summer,
a father at the snack counter low in the boat
gets breakfast for the others. *Here, let me drink some of*
Mom's coffee, so it won't be so full
for you to carry, he says to his son,
a boy of ten or eleven. The boat
lies lower and lower in the water as the last
cars drive on, it tilts its massive
grey floor like the flat world. Then the
screaming starts, *I carry four things,*
and I only give you one, and you drop it,
what are you, a baby? a high, male
shrieking, and it doesn't stop, *Are you two?*
Are you a baby? I give you one thing,
no one in the room seems to move for a second,
a steaming pool spreading on the floor, little
sea with its own waves, the boy
at the shore of it. *Can't you do anything*
right? Are you two? Are you two?, the piercing
cry of the father. *Go away,*
go up to your mother, get out of here—
the purser swabbing the floor, the boy
not moving from where the first word touched him,
and I could not quite walk past him, I paused
and said *I spilled my coffee on the deck, last trip,*
it happens to us all. He turned to me,
his lips everted so the gums gleamed,
he hissed a guttural hiss, and in
a voice like Gollum's or the Exorcist girl's when she
made the stream of vomit and beamed it
eight feet straight into the minister's mouth
he said *Shut up, shut up, shut up,* as if

protecting his father, peeling from himself
a thin wing of hate, and wrapping it
tightly around father and son, shielding them.

The Prepositions

When I started Junior High, I thought
I'd probably be a Behavior Problem
all my life, John Muir Grammar
the spawning grounds, the bad-seed bed, but
the first morning at Willard, the dawn
of 7th grade, they handed me a list
of forty-five prepositions, to learn
by heart. I stood in the central courtyard,
enclosed garden that grew cement,
my pupils followed the line of the arches
up and over, up and over, like
alpha waves, *about, above,*
across, along, among, around, an
odd comfort began, in me,
before, behind, below, beneath,
beside, between, I stood in that sandstone
square, and started to tame. *Down,*
from, in, into, near, I was
located there, watching the Moorish half-
circles rise and fall. *Off,*
on, onto, out, outside, we
came from 6th grades all over the city
to meet each other for the first time,
White tennis-club boys who did not
speak to me, White dorks
who did, Black student-council guys who'd gaze
off, above my head, and the Black
plump goof-off, who walked past and
suddenly flicked my sweater-front, I thought to shame me.
Over, past, since, through,
that was the year my father came home in the
middle of the night with those thick earthworms

of blood of his face, trilobites of
elegant gore, cornice and crisp
waist of the extinct form,
till, to, toward, under, the
lining of my uterus convoluted,
shapely and scarlet as the jointed leeches
of wound clinging to my father's face in that
mask, *unlike, until, up,* I'd
walk, day and night, into
the Eden of the list, *hortus enclosus* where
everything had a place. I was *in*
relation to, upon, with, and when I
got to forty-five I could start over,
pull the hood of the list down over
my brain again. It was the first rest
I had had from my mind. My glance would run
slowly along the calm electro-
cardiogram of adobe cloister,
within, without, I'd repeat the prayer I'd
received, a place in the universe,
meaningless but a place, an exact location—
Telegraph, Woolsey, Colby, Russell—
Berkeley, 1956,
fourteen, the breaking of childhood, beginning of memory.

1954

Then dirt scared me, because of the dirt
he had put on her face. And her training bra
scared me—the newspapers, morning and evening,
kept saying it, *training bra*,
as if the cups of it had been calling
the breasts up, he buried her in it,
perhaps he had never bothered to take it
off, and they had found her underpants
in a garbage can. And I feared the word
eczema, like my acne and like
the X in the paper which marked her body,
as if he had killed her for not being flawless.
I feared his name, Burton Abbott,
the first name that was a last name,
as if he was not someone specific.
It was nothing one could learn from his face.
His face was dull and ordinary,
it took away what I'd thought I could count on
about evil. He looked thin, and lonely,
it was horrifying, he looked almost humble.
I felt awe that dirt was so impersonal,
and pity for the training bra,
pity and terror of eczema.
And I could not sit on my mother's electric
blanket anymore, I began to have
a fear of electricity—
the good people, the parents, were going
to fry him to death. This was what
his parents had been telling us:
Burton Abbott, Burton Abbott,
death to the person, death to the home planet.
The worst thing would have been to think

of her, of what it had been to be her,
alive, to be walked, alive, into that cabin,
to look into those eyes, and see the human.

Cool Breeze

(for Joseph Davis Gilbert)

You talked to me a lot about your kid sister,
Rebecca, a.k.a. Reebabecka,
and you knew me as my sister's kid sister,
fourteen, and a late bloomer, and homely,
you talked to me about your family,
and your dream of cutting an LP,
and the Juniors and Sophomores you were in love with, or who
were in love with you, or who maybe you had slept with—
they were White, as I was, but you called me Miss Shary
Cobb, Miss Cool Breeze Herself.
You didn't mind I was in love with you,
you were Senior Class President.
And you would dance with me, astronomer
who pointed out to me the star
bright of the cervix, when we danced it became
exact to me, far inside me
in the night sky. And you would park with me,
you would draw my hand gently across you, you had
mercy on me, and on yourself. When you would
slide your hand up under my sweater,
my mouth would open, but I'd stop you, and you would
say, rather fondly, Protecting your sacred
virginity? And I would say Yes,
I could always tell you the truth.
When the White cops broke up the dance in your neighborhood,
your friends worked to get us out the back
unseen, if the cops saw us together
they would hurt someone. We crouched behind a hedge,
and I began to understand
you were less safe than me. Squatting
and whispering, I understood, as if
the bending of our bodies was teaching me,

that everyone was against you—the ones I had called
everyone, the White men
and the White women, the grown-ups, the blind
and deaf. And when you died, your LP cut,
and you had married the beauty from your neighborhood,
when you went off the coast road with your White
lover, into the wind off the ocean,
your Jag end over end, catching fire—
I knew that my hands were not free of your
blood, brother—Reebabecka's brother.

For and Against Knowledge

(for Christa MacAuliffe)

What happened to her? As long as it was she,
what did she see? Strapped in,
tilted back, so her back was toward
the planet she was leaving, feeling the Gs
press her with their enormous palm, did she
weep with excitement in the roar, and in
the lens of a tear glimpse for an instant
a disc of fire? If she were our daughter,
would I think about it, how she had died, was she
torn apart, was she burned—the way
I have wondered about the first seconds
of our girl's life, when she was a cell a
cell had just entered, she hung in me
a ball of grey liquid, without nerves,
without eyes or memory, it was
she, I love her. So I want to slow it
down, and take each millisecond
up, take her, at each point,
in my mind's arms—the first, final
shock hit, as if God touched
a thumb to her brain and it went out, like a mercy killing,
and then, when it was no longer she,
the flames came—as we burned my father
when he had left himself. Then the massive bloom un-
buckled and jumped, she was vaporized back
down to the level of the cell. And the spirit—
I have never understood the spirit,
all I know is the shape it takes,
the wavering flame of flesh. Those
who know about the spirit may tell you
where she is, and why. What I want
to do is to find every cell,

slip it out of the fishes' mouths,
ash in the tree, soot in our eyes
where she enters our lives, I want to play it
backwards, burning jigsaw puzzle
of flesh suck in its million stars
to meet, in the sky, boiling metal
fly back
together, and cool.
Pull that rocket
back down
surely to earth, open the hatch
and draw them out like fresh-born creatures,
sort them out, family by family, go
away, disperse, do not meet here.

The Spouses Waking Up in the Hotel Mirror

The man looked like himself, only more so,
his face lucent, his silence profound as if
inevitable, but the woman looked
like a different species from an hour before,
a sandhill crane or a heron, her eyes
skinned back, she looked insane with happiness.
After he got up, I looked at her,
lying on her back in the bed.
Her ribs and breasts and clavicles had
the molded look of a gladiator's
torso-armor, formal bulge of the
pectoral, forged nipple, her deltoid
heron-elongated,
I couldn't get her provenance
but the pelvic bone was wildly curled,
wrung, I could see she was a skeleton
in there, that hair on her body buoyant
though the woman was stopped completely, stilled as if
paralyzed. I looked at her face,
blood-darkened, it was a steady face,
I saw she was very good at staring
and could make up her mind to stare at me
until I would look away first.
I saw her bowled, suffused forehead,
her bony cheeks and jaws, I saw she could
watch her own house burn
without moving a muscle, I saw she could light
the pyre. She looked very much like her father, that
capillary-rich face, and very
much like her mother, the curlicues
at the corners of the features. She was very male
and very female,

very hermaphroditical,
I could see her in a temple, tying someone up
or being tied up, or being made nothing
or making someone nothing,
I saw she was full of cruelty
and full of kindness, brimming with it—
I had known but not known this, that she was human,
she had it all inside her, all of it.
She saw me seeing that, she liked that I saw it.
A full life—I saw her living it,
and then I saw her think of someone who
ignores her rather as her father ignored her,
and the clear, intransigent white of her eyes
went murky grey, the sections of her face pulled
away from each other like the continents
before they tore apart, long before they drifted.
I saw that she had been beaten, I saw her
looking away like a begging dog,
I averted my eyes, and turned my head
as the beloved came back, and came over to her
and came down to me, I looked into his iris
like looking at a rainstorm by moonrise, or a still
winter lake, just as its cleavages
take, or into crystal, when crystal
is forming, wet as nectar or milk
or semen, the first skein from a boy's heart.

You Kindly

Because I felt too weak to move
you kindly moved for me, kneeling
and turning, until you could take my breast-tip in the
socket of your lips, and my womb went down
on itself, drew sharply over and over
to its tightest shape, the way, when newborns
nurse, the fist of the uterus
with each, milk, tug, powerfully
shuts. I saw your hand, near me, your
daily hand, your thumbnail,
the quiet hairs on your fingers—to see your
hand its ordinary self, when your mouth at my
breast was drawing sweet gashes of come
up from my womb made black fork-flashes of a
celibate's lust shoot through me. And I couldn't
lift my head, and you swiveled, and came down
close to me, delicate blunt
touch of your hard penis in long
caresses down my face, species
happiness, calm which gleams
with fearless anguished desire. It found
my pouring mouth, the back of my throat,
and the bright wall which opens. It seemed to
take us hours to move the bone
creatures so their gods could be fitted to each other,
and then, at last, home, root
in the earth, wing in the air. As it finished,
it seemed my sex was a grey flower
the color of the brain, smooth and glistening,
a complex calla or iris which you
were creating with the errless digit
of your sex. But then, as it finished again,

one could not speak of a blossom, or the blossom
was stripped away, as if, until
that moment, the cunt had been clothed, still,
in the thinnest garment, and now was bare
or more than bare, silver wet-suit of
matter itself gone, nothing
there but the paradise flay. And then
more, that cannot be told—may be,
but cannot be, things that did not
have to do with me, as if some
wires crossed, and history
or war, or the witches possessed, or the end
of life were happening in me, or I was
in a borrowed body, I knew
what I could not know, did-was-done-to
what I cannot do-be-done-to, so when
we returned, I cried, afraid for a moment
I was dead, and had got my wish to come back,
once, and sleep with you, on a summer
afternoon, in an empty house
where no one could hear us.
I lowered the salt breasts of my eyes
to your mouth, and you sucked,
then I looked at your face, at its absence of unkindness,
its giving that absence off as a matter
I cannot name, I was seeing not you
but something that lives between us, that can live
only between us. I stroked back the hair in
pond and sex rivulets
from your forehead, gently raked it back
along your scalp,
I did not think of my father's hair

in death, those oiled paths, I lay
along your length and did not think how he
did not love me, how he trained me not to be loved.

Where Will Love Go?

Where will love go? When my father
died, and my love could no longer shine
on the oily, drink-contused slopes of his skin,
then my love for him lived inside me,
and lived wherever the fog they made of him
coiled like a spirit. And when I die
my love for him will live in my vapor
and live in my children, some of it
still rubbed into the grain of the desk my father left me
and the oxblood pores of the leather chair which he
sat in, in a stupor, when I was a child, and then
gave me passionately after his death—our
souls seem locked in it, together,
two alloys in a metal, and we're there
in the black and chrome workings of his forty-pound
1932 Underwood,
the trapezes stilled inside it on the desk
in front of the chair. Even when the children
have died, our love will live in their children
and still be here in the arm of the chair,
locked in it, like the secret structure of matter,

but what if we ruin everything,
the earth burning like a human body,
storms of soot wreathing it
in permanent winter? Where will love go?
Will the smoke be made of animal love,
will the clouds of roasted ice, circling
the globe, be all that is left of love,
will the sphere of cold, turning ash,
seen by no one, heard by no one,
hold all

our love? Then love
is powerless, and means nothing.

The Protestor

(for Bob Stein)

We were driving north, through the snow, you said
you had turned twenty-one during Vietnam, you were
1-A. The road curved
and curved back, the branches laden,
you said you had decided not to go
to Canada. Which meant you'd decided to
go to jail, a slender guy of
twenty-one, which meant you'd decided to be
raped rather than to kill, if it was their
life or your ass, it was your ass.
We drove in silence, such soft snow
so heavy borne-down. That was when I'd come to
know I loved the land of my birth—
when the men had to leave, they could never come back,
I looked and loved every American
needle on every American tree, I thought
my soul was in it. But if I were taken and
used, taken and used, I think
my soul would die, I think I'd be easily broken,
the work of my life over. And you'd said,
This is the work of my life, to say,
with my body itself, You fuckers you cannot
tell me who to kill. As if there were a
spirit free of the body, safe from it.
After a while, you talked about your family,
not starting, as I had, with
husband and kids, leaving everyone else out—
you started with your grandparents
and worked your way back, away from yourself,
deeper and deeper into Europe, into
the Middle East, the holy book
buried sometimes in the garden, sometimes
swallowed and carried in the ark of the body itself.

The Summer-Camp Bus Pulls Away from the Curb

Whatever he needs, he has or doesn't
have by now.
Whatever the world is going to do to him
it has started to do. With a pencil and two
Hardy Boys and a peanut butter sandwich and
grapes he is on his way, there is nothing
more we can do for him. Whatever is
stored in his heart, he can use, now.
Whatever he has laid up in his mind
he can call on. What he does not have
he can lack. The bus gets smaller and smaller, as one
folds a flag at the end of a ceremony,
onto itself, and onto itself, until
only a triangle wedge remains.
Whatever his exuberant soul
can do for him, it is doing right now.
Whatever his arrogance can do
it is doing to him. Everything
that's been done to him, he will now do.
Everything that's been placed in him will
come out, now, the contents of a trunk
unpacked and lined up on a bunk in the underpine light.

The Talkers

All week, we talked. Born in the same
year and hospital we had so much to catch
up on we couldn't stop, we talked
in the morning on the porch, when I combed my hair
and flung the comb-hair out into the air, and it
floated down the slope, toward the valley.
We talked while walking to the car, talked
over its mild, belled roof,
while opening the doors, then ducked down
and there we were, bent toward the interior, talking.
Meeting, in the middle of the day,
the first thing when we saw each other
we opened our mouths. All day,
we sang to each other the level music
of spoken language. Even while we ate
we did not pause, I'd speak to him through
the broken body of the butter cookie,
gently spraying him with crumbs. We talked
and walked, we leaned against the opposite sides of the
car and talked in the parking lot until
everyone had driven off, we clung to its
maroon raft and started a new subject.
We did not talk about his wife, much,
or my husband, but to everything else
we turned the workings of our lips and tongues
—up to our necks in the hot tub, or
walking up the steep road,
stepping into the hot dust as if
down into the ions of a wing, and on the
sand, next to each other, as we turned
the turns that upon each other would have been the
turnings of joy—even under

water there trailed from our mouths the delicate
chains of our sentences. But mostly at night, and
far into the night, we talked until we
dropped, as if, stopping for an instant, we might have
moved right toward each other. Today,
he said he felt he could talk to me forever,
it must be the way the angels live,
sitting across from each other, deep
in the bliss of their shared spirit. My God,
they are not going to touch each other.

First Thanksgiving

When she comes back, from college, I will see
the skin of her upper arms, cool,
matte, glossy. She will hug me, my old
soupy chest against her breasts,
I will smell her hair! She will sleep in this apartment,
her sleep like an untamed, good object, like a
soul in a body. She came into my life the
second great arrival, fresh
from the other world—which lay, from within him,
within me. Those nights, I fed her to sleep,
week after week, the moon rising,
and setting, and waxing—whirling, over the months,
in a steady blur, around our planet.
Now she doesn't need love like that, she has
had it. She will walk in glowing, we will talk,
and then, when she's fast asleep, I'll exult
to have her in that room again,
behind that door! As a child, I caught
bees, by the wings, and held them, some seconds,
looked into their wild faces,
listened to them sing, then tossed them back
into the air—I remember the moment the
arc of my toss swerved, and they entered
the corrected curve of their departure.

The Native

This touching of him, on the borders of sleep,
my sternum and hipbones fitted to his tapered
back, my lap curled to his buttocks,
folded around them like a wing with an umber
eye-spot,
it feels to me like the most real thing,
my hand like elements on him, like
the waters stroking along him inside
his mother, without language, his large
eyes unsated ungrieving not even conscious yet,
the wind traveling the contours of the world,
a wind that comes when those who loved
the dead are allowed to touch them again. This feels like
who I am, I am the caressing of him,
and maybe especially this caressing,
gentle sweeping at the borders of sex,
sweeper of its sills in half-sleep, I
am the curve of his buttock, supple fork-
lightning of each hair, follicle
and pore, and the underlying bone,
the death-god of the skeleton,
and the intricate, thrilling anus, like a
character on a landscape, knob-end
of one of the long drool-bones of the spirit
running the length of the body, and then—
but when we cross from the back of the body
under, then this is over, till the next
morning or night when it is back again,
my home, colorless bliss, which I quietly
walk. I saw it in the Bible, in a sideways
oval, sepia and white, the hills
of the peaceable kingdom, its stream and live oak,

my eyes strolled it, and now my hand
walks, to and fro in the earth
and up and down in it, I am opposite-
Satan, I do not want to rule,
only to praise. I think I did not
want to be born,
I did not want to be conceived,
I held to nothing, to its dense parental
fur. Slowly I was pulled away,
but I would not let go, perhaps they had to
knock me off with a stick like someone
clinging to a live, downed wire,
I came away with the skin of the other
world on my palms, and at night, when I touch him,
wander on him, hold to him, and move
on and hold to him, I feel I am home again.

The Knowing

Afterwards, when we have slept, paradise-
comaed, and woken, we lie a long time
looking at each other.
I do not know what he sees, but I see
eyes of quiet evenness
and endurance, a patience like the dignity
of matter. I love the open ocean
blue-grey-green of his iris, I love
the curve of it against the white,
that curve the sight of what has caused me
to come, when he's quite still, deep
inside me. I have never seen a curve
like that, except our sphere, from outer
space. I don't know where he got
his steadiness as if without self-regard,
almost without self, and yet
he chose one woman, instead of the others.
By knowing him, I get to know
the purity of the animal
which mates for life. Sometimes he is slightly
smiling, but mostly he just gazes at me gazing,
his entire face lit. I love
to see it change if I cry—there is no worry,
no pity, a graver radiance. If we
are on our backs, side by side,
with our faces turned fully to face each other,
I can hear a tear from my lower eye
hit the sheet, as if it is an early day on earth,
and then the upper eye's tears
braid and sluice down through the lower eyebrow
like the invention of farming, irrigation, a non-nomadic people.
I am so lucky that I can know him.

This is the only way to know him.
I am the only one who knows him.
When I wake again, he is still looking at me,
as if he is eternal. For an hour
we wake and doze, and slowly I know
that though we are sated, though we are hardly
touching, this is the coming that the other
brought us to the edge of—we are entering,
deeper and deeper, gaze by gaze,
this place beyond the other places,
beyond the body itself, we are making
love.

from *The Unswept Room*

Kindergarten Abecedarian

I thought what I had to do was to read
the very long word, over the chalkboard,
ab-ke*dev*-gi-*hij*-klem-*nop*-qurs-
tuv-wix-*yiz*, but what I had to do
was to look at a crescent moon-shape and to go
k k k k with my mind. It was strange,
like other things—that a very large Boy owned everything,
even a fire, where he could put me for the thoughts
in my head. Each day, I tried to read
the world, to find his name in it,
the trees bending in cursive, the bees
looping their sky script. Crescent moon
was *k-k-k*. Cereal bowl
uh-uh-uh. Cap-gun *puh-*
puh-puh. *K-k, uh-uh, puh-puh*,
kk-uhh-puhh, kk-uhh-puhh—
cup. Would God be mad? I had made
a false cup, in my mind, and although
he had made my mind, and owned it, maybe this was
not his cup, maybe he could not
put this cup in hell, and make it
scream the cup-scream. Maybe the paper
world was ours, as the actual one was his—
I was becoming a reader. For a moment I almost remember it,
when I stood back, on the other side
of the alphabet, *a*-b-*c*-d-
e-f-*g*, and took that first
step in, *h*-i-*j*-k
l-m-n-o-*p*, and stood astride
the line of the border of literacy,
q-r-*s*, *t*-u-*v*,
I would work for a life of this, I would ask
sanctuary: *w, x, y, z*.

Bible Study: 71 B.C.E.

After Marcus Licinius Crassus
defeated the army of Spartacus,
he crucified 6,000 men.
That is what the records say,
as if he drove in the 18,000
nails himself. I wonder how
he felt, that day, if he went outside
among them, if he walked that human
woods. I think he stayed in his tent
and drank, and maybe copulated,
hearing the singing being done for him,
the woodwind-tuning he was doing at one
remove, to the six-thousandth power.
And maybe he looked out, sometimes,
to see the rows of instruments,
his orchard, the earth bristling with it
as if a patch in his brain had itched
and this was his way of scratching it
directly. Maybe it gave him pleasure,
and a sense of balance, as if he had suffered,
and now had found redress for it,
and voice for it. I speak as a monster,
someone who today has thought at length
about Crassus, his ecstasy of feeling
nothing while so much is being
felt, his hot lightness of spirit
in being free to walk around
while other are nailed above the earth.
It may have been the happiest day
of his life. If he had suddenly cut
his hand on a wineglass, I doubt he would
have woken up to what he was doing.

It is frightening to think of him suddenly
seeing what he was, to think of him running
outside, to try to take them down,
one man to save 6,000.
If he could have lowered one,
and seen the eyes when the level of pain
dropped like a sudden soaring into pleasure,
wouldn't that have opened in him
the wild terror of understanding
the other? But then he would have had
5,999
to go. Probably it almost never
happens, that a Marcus Crassus
wakes. I think he dozed, and was roused
to his living dream, lifted the flap
and stood and looked out, at the rustling, creaking
living field—his, like an external
organ, a heart.

5¢ a Peek

The day my class was to go to the circus,
I sidled into the bathroom, early,
and stood on tiptoe, up into the bottom
corner of the mirror, and leaned on the sink,
and slowly cut off my eyelashes
down close to the eyelid. I had no idea what I was
doing, or why, I studied the effect
—not bad, a little stark—but when I saw the effect
on my mother, not just anger, but pity
and horror, I was interested.
I think I had almost given up on being
a girl, on trying to grow up to be a woman like my mother,
I wanted to get disadopted
and go home to be the baby with the calf's head,
home to my birth-mother the bearded lady,
my father the sword swallower stopped mid-swallow,
one with the sword. I had tried to act normal,
but when the inspiration came
I felt I was meant to act on it,
to look at my mom with my gaze trimmed to a seer's
and see her see me for an instant, see
her irises contract. I did not
imagine I could ever leave my mother,
mostly I *was* her, in distorted form,
but at least for that second the itsy scissors
spoke to her with their birdy beak,
skreeek, skreeek, witch whinge. And when
my lashes grew back, no thicker no thinner no
shorter no longer, my mother sat me
down, and taught me to bat them, to look
sidelong, blindly, and shudder them at seven beats a second.

Grey Girl

(for Yusef Komunyakaa and Toi Derricotte)

We were walking down Park, on the grates over
the exhaust ducts of the lavish apartments,
we were walking on air, on iron bars,
three abreast—four breasts,
two on either side of the man
who had survived through various wars,
my friend and I proud to walk him through the
evening after his reading. Our skirts
faffled, we were tall, we were his color guard, his
woman of color and woman of no
color guard, we were talking about
family and race, and a greed or lust
rose in me to talk about
disliking myself. I was crouching slightly,
spider-dancing over hot air, and I
said, You want to know about white people?
I'll tell you about white people,
I lived in close proximity to them
and I *was* them, that meanness they used on me
was what I was made of. Out of the corner of my
eye, I glimpsed myself for a second
in a store window, a swirl of grey, a
thirster after substance. My companions became
quiet, as if they had pulled back,
a bit, and were holding still, with wary
courtesy. In that second, I could almost
sense myself, whuffolk amok,
one who wanted to win something
in the war of the family, to rant in the faces
of the war-struck about her home-front pain.
It is hard to see oneself as dangerous
and stupid, but what I had said was true,

the people who had hurt me most were my makers,
but there had not been what I saw now as a ring
of haters around us, encircling us.
I had a flash of knowledge of this
on the sidewalk—as we kept going, I sensed
two, living beings, and one half-
idiot, a grey girl walking. Who did she
think she was, to relish herself
for hating herself, to savor, proudly,
the luxury of hating her own people?
All evening, I looked at my friends'
womanly beauty, and manly beauty,
and the table with its wines, and meats, and fruits,
and flowers, as if we could go back to the beginning.

Still Life in Landscape

It was night, it had rained, there were pieces of cars and
half-cars strewn, it was still, and bright,
a woman was lying on the highway, on her back,
with her head curled back and tucked under her shoulders
so the back of her head touched her spine
between her shoulder blades, her clothes
mostly accidented off, and her
leg gone, a tall bone
sticking out of the stub of her thigh—
this was her abandoned matter,
my mother grabbed my head and turned it and
clamped it into her chest, between
her breasts. My father was driving—not sober
but not in this accident, we'd approached it out of
neutral twilight, broken glass
on wet black macadam, an underlying
midnight abristle with stars. This was
the world—maybe the only one.
The dead woman was not the person
my father had recently almost run over,
who had suddenly leapt away from our family
car, jerking back from death,
she was not I, she was not my mother,
but maybe she was a model of the mortal,
the elements ranged around her on the tar—
glass, bone, metal, flesh, and the family.

The Wedding Vow

I did not stand at the altar, I stood
at the foot of the chancel steps, with my beloved,
and the minister stood on the top step
holding the open Bible. The church
was wood, painted ivory inside, no people—God's
stable perfectly cleaned. It was night,
spring—outside, a moat of mud,
and inside, from the rafters, flies
fell onto the open Bible, and the minister
tilted it and brushed them off. We stood
beside each other, crying slightly
with fear and awe. In truth, we had married
that first night, in bed, we had been
married by our bodies, but now we stood
in history—what our bodies had said,
mouth to mouth, we now said publicly,
gathered together, death. We stood
holding each other by the hand, yet I also
stood as if alone, for a moment,
just before the vow, though taken
years before, took. It was a vow
of the present and the future, and yet I felt it
to have some touch on the distant past
or the distant past on it, I felt
the wordless, dry, crying ghost of my
parents' marriage there, somewhere
in the echoing space—perhaps one of the
plummeting flies, bouncing slightly
as it hit *forsaking all others*, then was brushed
away. I felt as if I had come
to claim a promise—the sweetness I'd inferred
from their sourness, and at the same time that I

had come, congenitally unworthy, to beg.
And yet, I had been working toward this hour
all my life. And then it was time
to speak—he was offering me, no matter
what, his life. That is all I had to
do, that evening, to accept the gift
I had longed for—to say I had accepted it,
as if being asked if I breathe. Do I take?
I do. I take as he takes—we have been
practicing this. Do you bear this pleasure? I do.

His Costume

Somehow I never stopped to notice
that my father liked to dress as a woman.
He had his sign language about women
talking too much, and being stupid,
but whenever there was a costume party
he would dress like us, the tennis balls
for breasts—balls for breasts—the pageboy
blond wig, the lipstick, he would sway
his body with moves of gracefulness
as if one being could be the whole
universe, its ends curving back to come
up from behind it. Six feet, and maybe
one-eighty, one-ninety, he had the shapely
legs of a male Grable—in a short
skirt, he leaned against a bookcase pillar
nursing his fifth drink, gazing
around from inside his mascara purdah
with those salty eyes. The woman from next door
had a tail and ears, she was covered with Reynolds Wrap,
she was Kitty Foil, and my mother was in
a teeny tuxedo, but he always won
the prize. Those nights, he had a look of daring,
as if he was getting away with something,
a look of triumph, of having stolen
back. And as far as I knew, he never threw
up as a woman, or passed out, or made
those signals of scorn with his hands, just leaned,
voluptuous, at ease, deeply
present, as if sensing his full potential, crossing
over into himself, and back,
over and back.

First Weeks

Those first weeks, I hardly knew how to
love our daughter. Her face looked crushed,
crumpled with worry—and not even
despairing, but just disheartened, a look of
endurance. The skin of her face was finely
wrinkled, there were wisps of hair on her ears,
she looked a little like a squirrel, suspicious,
tranced. And smallish, 6.13,
wizened—she looked as if she were wincing
away from me without moving. The first
moment I had seen her, my glasses off,
in the delivery room, a blur of blood
and blue skin, and limbs, I had known her,
upside down, and they righted her, and there
came that faint, almost sexual, wail, and her
whole body flushed rose.
When I saw her next, she was bound in cotton,
someone else had cleaned her, wiped
the inside of my body off her
and combed her hair in narrow scary
plough-lines. She was ten days early,
sleepy, the breast engorged, standing out nearly
even with the nipple, her lips would so much as
approach it, it would hiss and spray.
And when we took her home, she shrieked
and whimpered, like a dream of a burn victim,
and when she was quiet, she would lie there and peer, not quite
anxiously. I didn't blame her,
she'd been born to my mother's daughter. I would kneel
and gaze at her, and pity her.
All day I nursed her, all night I walked her,
and napped, and nursed, and walked her. And then,

one day, she looked at me, as if
she knew me. She lay along my forearm, fed, and
gazed at me as if remembering me,
as if she had known me, and liked me, and was getting
her memory back. When she smiled at me,
delicate rictus like a birth-pain coming,
I fell in love, I became human.

The Clasp

She was four, he was one, it was raining, we had colds,
we had been in the apartment two weeks straight,
I grabbed her to keep her from shoving him over on his
face, again, and when I had her wrist
in my grasp I compressed it, fiercely, for almost a
second, to make an impression on her,
to hurt her, our beloved firstborn, I even nearly
savored the stinging sensation of the squeezing, the
expression, into her, of my anger,
"Never, never again," the righteous
chant accompanying the clasp. It happened very
fast—grab, crush, crush,
crush, release—and at the first extra
force, she swung her head, as if checking
who this was, and looked at me,
and saw me—yes, this was her mom,
her mom was doing this. Her dark,
deeply open eyes took me
in, she knew me, in the shock of the moment
she learned me. This was her mother, one of the
two whom she most loved, the two
who loved her most, near the source of love
was this.

Diaphragm Aria

It's curious and sweet to slip it out
and look inside, to see what's there,
like a treasure hunt, dimestore toys
and dolls tucked into the root-floor of the woods,
or tilt up a stone in the yard and find,
in the groove of her path, the flame-brown newt. Now I
read the shallow cup of dregs,
shreds like clothes torn away in
eagerness, cloth of the bodies, which rips
to a cloud of threads. Here our daughter
never picked her finicky way,
here our son never somersaulted,
here only our not-children
advanced, and dropped, and surged forward
and were cut down, there a coil
of tail, here a ladyfinger, a
curl, a bone of the twin. When I have reached
into myself, and glistened out the dome,
I search its planetarium sky
for its weather, ivory nimbus, reach
of summer showers—these are the heavens
under which the grateful bodies
went to earth, dense with contentment,
moving, together, for those hour-long
moments, in a mattery paradise,
I gaze into the cumulus
of spermicide, I bless the lollers who
stay in that other sphere as we come
like surf on the shore of it.

The Window

Our daughter calls me, in tears—like water
being forced, under great pressure, from densest
stone. *I am mad at you,* she whispers.
You said in a poem that you're a survivor,
that's O.K., but you said that you are
a Jew, when you're not, that's so cheap. You're right,
I say, you're so right. *Did you see the Holocaust*
movie, she asks, in a stifled voice,
there's a window on the third floor of the barracks
and I know it's a little bathroom, I used it
in Poland the day I was there, and she sobs,
a sound like someone swallowing gravel.
And the rooms hadn't been dusted, it was
as if everything was left as it was,
and some of the same molecules
might be there in the room. And there were exhibit cases,
one with hair—hair. In my mind
I see the landscape, behind glass,
the human hills and mountains, the intimate
crowning of a private life
now a case of clouds, detritus,
meshes. *And there were eyeglasses,*
a huge pile of liking to read,
and of liking books, and being able to see, and
then . . . then there was a display case
of suitcases, and an Orthodox guide was
taking a tour through. She is able, while she cries,
to speak, in a compressed, stopped-down voice
as if a pebble could talk. *He was telling*
a big class of Bar Mitzvah boys
to look at the names on the suitcases—
some of them had believed . . . they were going . . .

on vacation, she says—or something like it.
I cannot hear each word
but sometimes just the creak of rock
on water. I do not want to ask her
to repeat. She seems to be saying she had to
leave the room, to find a place
to cry in, maybe the little bathroom,
I feel as if I am there, near her,
and am seeing, through her, the horror of the human,
as if she is transparent, holding
no gaze to herself. *There were people not
crying, just looking,* she says, then she says
so much about us is unbearable.
We talk an hour, we are coming back
up as if from inside the ground,
I try to tell her it was not weakness
in her, that it was love she felt,
the helplessness of each life, and the
dread of our species. *Yeah yeah,* she says,
in the low voice of someone lately
the young in the nest, maybe soon
the nesting one—and that hour, within
her view, the evidence of the wish
that the ark be consumed—and no thought of herself
to distract her, nothing distracts her, not even
the breathing of her own body as she sees.

Fish Oil

One midnight, home late from work,
the apartment reeked of fish boiled
in oil. All the windows were shut,
and all the doors were open—up
from the pan and spatula rose a thick
helix of cod and olive. My husband
slept. I opened the windows and shut
the doors and put the plates in the sink
and oodled Palmolive all over. The next
day I fishwifed to a friend, and she said,
Someone might live with that, and come to
love the smell of a fry. And that evening,
I looked at my beloved, and who he is
touched me in the core of my heart. I sought
a bottle of extra-extra virgin,
and a recipe for sea fillet in
olive-branch juice, I filled the rooms with
swirls of finny perfume, the outlines
in the sand the early Christians drew,
the loop meaning safety, meaning me too,
I remembered my parents' frowns at any
whiff of savor outside the kitchen,
the Calvinist shudder, in that house, at the sweet
grease of life. I had come to my mate
a shocked being, agog, a salt
dab in his creel, girl in oil,
his dish. I had not known that one
could approve of someone entirely—one could
wake to the pungent day, one could awake
from the dream of judgment.

Wonder as Wander

At dusk, on those evenings she does not go out,
my mother potters around her house.
Her daily helpers are gone, there is no one
there, no one to tell what to do,
she wanders, sometimes she talks to herself,
fondly scolding, sometimes she suddenly
throws out her arms and screams—high notes
lying here and there on the carpets
like bodies touched by a downed wire,
she journeys, she quests, she marco-polos through
the gilded gleamy loot-rooms, who is she.
I feel, now, that I do not know her,
and for all my staring, I have not seen her
—like the song she sang, when we were small,
I wonder as I wander, out under the sky,
how Jesus, the Savior, was born for, to die,
for poor lonely people, like you, and like I
—on the slow evenings alone, when she delays
and delays her supper, walking the familiar
halls past the mirrors and night windows,
I wonder if my mother is tasting a life
beyond this life—not heaven, her late
beloved is absent, her father absent,
and her staff is absent, maybe this is earth
alone, as she had not experienced it,
as if she is one of the poor lonely people,
as if she is born to die. I hold fast
to the thought of her, wandering in her house,
a luna moth in a chambered cage.
Fifty years ago, I'd squat in her
garden, with her Red Queens, and try
to sense the flyways of the fairies as they kept

the pollen flowing on its local paths,
and our breaths on their course of puffs—they kept
our eyes wide with seeing what we
could see, and not seeing what we could not see.

The Shyness

Then, when we were joined, I became
shyer. I became completed, joyful,
and shyer. I may have shone more, reflected
more, and from deep inside there rose
some glow passing steadily through me, but I was not
playing, now, I felt like someone
small, in a raftered church, or in
a cathedral, the vaulted spaces of the body
like a sacred woods. I was quiet when my throat was not
making those iron, orbital, earth,
rusted, noises at the hinge of matter and
whatever is not matter. He takes me
into the endings like another world at the
center of this one, and then, if he begins to
end when I am resting and I do not rejoin him yet
then I feel awe, I almost feel
fear, sometimes for a moment I feel
I should not move, or make a sound, as
if he is alone, now,
howling in the wilderness,
and yet I know we are in this place
together. I thought, now is the moment
I could become more loving, and my hands moved shyly
over him, secret as heaven,
and my mouth spoke, and in my beloved's
voice, by the bones of my head, the fields
groaned, and then I joined him again,
not shy, not bold, released, entering
the true home, where the trees bend down along the
ground and yet stand, then we lay together
panting as if saved from some disaster, and for ceaseless
instants, it came to pass what I have

heard about, it came to me
that I did not know I was separate
from this man, I did not know I was lonely.

April, New Hampshire

(for Jane Kenyon and Donald Hall)

Outside the door, a tiny narcissus
had come up through leaf mold. In the living room,
the old butterscotch collie let me
get my hand into the folds
of the mammal, and knead it. Inside their room
Don said, *This is it, this is where*
we lived and died. To the center of the maple
painted headboard—sleigh of beauty,
sleigh of night—there was an angel affixed
as if bound to it, with her wings open.
The bed spoke, as if to itself,
it sang. The whole room sang,
and the house, and the curve of the hill, like the curve between
a throat and a shoulder, sang, in praising
grief, and the ground, almost, rang,
hollowed-out bell waiting for its tongue
to be lowered in. At the grave site,
next to the big, smoothed, beveled,
felled, oak home, like the bole
of a Druid *duir*—inside it what comes not
close to being like who she was—
he stood, beside, in a long silence,
minutes, like the seething harness-creaking
when the water of a full watering is feeding
down into the ground, and he looked at us,
at each one, and he seemed not just
a person seeing people, he looked
almost another species, an eagle
gazing at eagles, fierce, intent,
wordless, eyelidless, seeing each one,
seeing deep
into each—

miles, years—he seemed to be Jane,
looking at us for the last time
on earth.

The Untangling

Detritus, in uncorrected
nature, in streambeds or on woods floors,
I have wanted to untangle, soft talon
of moss from twig, rabbit hair
from thorn from down. Often they come
in patches, little mattednesses,
I want to part their parts, trillium-
spadix, mouse-fur, chokecherry-needle,
granite-chip, I want to unbind them and
restore them to their living forms—I am
a housewife of conifer tide-pools, a parent who would
lift parents up off children, lissome
serpent of my mother's hair discoiled
from within my ear, wall of her tear with-
drawn Red-brown Sea from my hair—she to be
she; I, I. I love
to not know
what is my beloved
and what is I, I love for my I
to die, leaving the slack one, bliss-
pacified, to sleep with him
and wake, and sleep, rageless. Limb
by limb by lip by lip by sex by
sparkle of salt we part, hour by
hour we disentangle and dry,
and then, I relish to reach down
to that living nest that love has woven
bits of feather, and kiss-fleck, and
vitreous floater, and mica-glint, and no
snakeskin into, nectar-caulk and the
solder of sperm and semen dried
to knotted frog-clasps, which I break, gently,

groaning, and the world of the sole one unfastens
up, a lip folded back on itself
unfurls, murmurs, the postilion hairs
crackle, and the thin glaze overall—
glaucous as the pressed brooch
of mucus that quivered upright on my father's
tongue at death—crazes and shatters,
the garden tendrils out in its rows and
furrows, quaint, dented, archaic,
sweet of all perfume, pansy, peony,
dusk, starry, inviolate.

The Learner

When my mother tells me she has found her late husband's
flag in the attic, and put it up,
over the front door, for her party,
her voice on the phone is steady with the truth
of yearning, she sounds like a soldier who has known
no other life. For a moment I forget
the fierce one who raised me. We talk about her sweetheart,
how she took such perfect care of him
after his strokes. *And when the cancer came,*
it was BLACK, she says, and then it was WHITE.
—What? What do you mean? —It was BLACK, it was
cancer, it was terrible,
but he did not know to be afraid, and then it
took him mercifully, it was WHITE.
—Mom, I say, breaking a cold
sweat. *Could I say something, and you not*
get mad? Silence. I have never said anything
to question her. I'm shaking so the phone
is beating on my jaw. *—Yes . . . —Mom,*
people have kind of stopped saying that, BLACK for bad,
WHITE for good. —Well, I'M not a racist,
she says, with some of the plummy, almost sly
pride I have heard in myself. *—Well I think*
everyone is, Mom, but that's not
the point—if someone Black heard you,
how would they feel? —But no one Black
is here! she cries, and I say, *—Well then think of me*
as Black. It's quiet, then I say, *—It's like some of the*
things the kids are always telling me now,
"Mom, nobody says that any
more." And my mother says, in a soft
voice, with the timing of a dream, *—I'll never*

say that any more. And then, almost
anguished, *I PROMISE you that I'll never
say it again.* —*Oh, Mom,* I say, *don't
promise me, who am I,
you're doing so well, you're an amazing learner,*
and that is when, from inside my mother,
the mother of my heart speaks to me,
the one under the coloratura,
the alto, the woman under the child—who lay
under, waiting, all my life,
to speak—her low voice slowly
undulating, like the flag of her love,
she says, *Before, I, die, I am, learning,
things, I never, thought, I'd know, I am so
fortunate.* And then *They are things
I would not, have learned, if he, had lived,
but I cannot, be glad, he died,* and then
the sound of quiet crying, as if
I hear, near a clearing, a spirit of mourning
bathing itself, and singing.

Heaven to Be

When I'd picture my death, I would be lying on my back,
and my spirit would rise to my belly-skin and out
like a sheet of wax paper the shape of a girl, furl
over from supine to prone and like the djinn's
carpet begin to fly, low,
over our planet—heaven to be
unhurtable, and able to see without
cease or stint or stopperage,
to lie on the air, and look, and look,
not so different from my life, I would be
sheer with an almost not sore loneness,
looking at the earth as if seeing the earth
were my version of having a soul. But then
I could see my beloved, sort of standing
beside a kind of door in the sky—
not the door to the constellations,
to the pentangles, and borealis,
but a tidy flap at the bottom of the door in the
sky, like a little cat-door in the door,
through which is nothing. And he is saying to me that he must
go, now, it is time. And he does not
ask me, to go with him, but I feel
he would like me with him. And I do not think
it is a living nothing, where nonbeings
can make a kind of unearthly love, I
think it's the nothing kind of nothing, I think
we go through the door and vanish together.
What depth of joy to take his arm,
pressing it against my breast
as lovers do in a formal walk,
and take that step.

The Tending

My parents did not consider it, for me,
yet I can see myself in the woods of some other
world, with the aborted. It is early evening,
the air is ashen as if from funeral-home
chimneys, and there are beginnings of people
almost growing—but not changing—on stalks,
some in cloaks, or lady's-slippers,
others on little trellises.
Maybe I am one of the gardeners here,
we water them with salt water.
I recall the girl who had a curl
right in the middle of her forehead,
when she was good she was very very good, I was not like that,
when she was bad she was horrid, I am here
as if in a garden of the horrid—I move
and tend, by attention, to the rows, I think of
Mary Mary Quite Contrary
and feel I am seeing the silver bells
set down clapperless, the cockleshells
with the cockles eaten. And yet this is
a holy woods. When I think of the house
I came to, and the houses these brothers and sisters
might have come to, and what they might have
done with what was done there,
I wonder if some here have done,
by their early deaths, a boon of absence
to someone in the world. So I tend them, I hate
for them to remain thankless. I do not
sign to them—their lullaby
long complete,
I just walk, as if this were a kind of home,
a mothers' and fathers' place, and I am

among the sung who will not sing,
the harmed who will not harm.

Psalm

Bending over, at the August table
where the summer towels are kept, putting
a stack on the bottom shelf, I felt his
kiss, in its shock of whiskers, on an inner
curve of that place I know by his knowing,
have seen with the vision of his touch. To be entered
thus, on a hip-high table piled with
sheaves of towels, bath and hand,
terry-cloth eden, is to feel at one's center
a core of liquid heat as if
one is an earth. Some time later,
we were kissing in near sleep, *I think*
we did it this time, I whispered, *I think*
we're joined at the hip. He has a smile sometimes
from the heart; at this hour, I live in its light.
I gnaw very gently on his jaw, *Would you want me to*
eat you, in the Andes, in a plane crash, I murmur,
to survive? Yes. We smile. He asks,
Would you want me to eat you to survive? I would love it,
I cry out. We almost sleep, there is a series of
arms around us and between us, in sets,
touches given as if received. *Did you think*
we were going to turn into each other?, and I get
one of those smiles, as if his face
is a speckled, rubbled, sandy, satiny
cactus-flower eight inches across.
Yes, he whispers. I know he is humoring,
rote sweet-talking. A sliver of late
sun is coming through, between the curtains,
it illumines the scaly surfaces
of my knuckles, its line like a needle held,
to cleanse it, above a match. I move

my wedding finger to stand in the slit
of flame. From the ring's curve there rises
a fan of borealis fur
like the first instant of sunrise. Do not
tell me this could end. Do not tell me.

The Unswept

Broken bay leaf. Olive pit.
Crab leg. Claw. Crayfish armor.
Whelk shell. Mussel shell. Dogwinkle. Snail.
Wishbone tossed unwished on. Test
of sea urchin. Chicken foot.
Wrasse skeleton. Hen head,
eye shut, beak open as if
singing in the dark. Laid down in tiny
tiles, by the rhyparographer,
each scrap has a shadow—each shadow cast
by a different light. Permanently fresh
husks of the feast! When the guest has gone,
the morsels dropped on the floor are left
as food for the dead—O my characters,
my imagined, here are some fancies of crumbs
from under love's table.

A NOTE ABOUT THE AUTHOR

Sharon Olds was born in San Francisco, and educated at Stanford and Columbia. Her first book, *Satan Says*, received the inaugural San Francisco Poetry Center Award. Her second, *The Dead and the Living*, was the Lamont Poetry Selection for 1983 and the winner of the National Book Critics Circle Award. *The Father* was shortlisted for the T. S. Eliot Prize in England. Sharon Olds was the New York State Poet for 1998 to 2000. She teaches poetry workshops in the Graduate Creative Writing Program at New York University, and helped to found the N.Y.U. workshop program at Goldwater Hospital on Roosevelt Island. Her most recent book, *The Unswept Room*, was a finalist for the National Book Award and the National Book Critics Circle Award. She was the James Merrill Fellow of the Academy of American Poets for 2003 and has just been named a Fellow of the American Academy of Arts & Sciences. She lives in New York City.

A NOTE ON THE TYPE

The text of this book was set in a typeface called Bell. The original punches for this face were cut in 1788 by the engraver Richard Austin for the typefoundry of John Bell (1745–1831), the most outstanding typographer of his day. They are the earliest English "modern" type design, and show the influence of French copperplate engraving and the work of the Fournier and Didot families. However, the Bell face has a distinct identity of its own, and might also be classified as a delicate and refined rendering of Scotch Roman.

Composed by NK Graphics,
Keene, New Hampshire

Printed and bound by Berryville Graphics,
Berryville, Virginia

Designed by Soonyoung Kwon